INFLECTION
POINT

INFLECTION POINT

REDEFINING YOUR ROLE IN THE
INSURANCE AND FINANCIAL SERVICES INDUSTRY
WHEN THE EXISTING MODEL NO LONGER WORKS

TROY KORSGADEN

ISBN:
Print: 978-1-947505-20-9
Digital: 978-1-947505-21-6

Cover design and interior formatting by Anne McLaughlin, Blue Lake Design
Published in the United States by Baxter Press, Friendswood, Texas

Third Printing

Note: Content in Chapter 4, "Getting It Right," was previously published in
360 Property & Casualty, on September 10, 2019, in an article
by Troy Korsgaden titled, "Simple Strategies for Creating
Great Customer Experience."
Content in Chapter 8, "Lifelong Learning," is adapted from a blog in
Selling Power Magazine. These concepts are also found in Insurance News.

CONTENTS

INTRODUCTION
WE'VE REACHED THE INFLECTION POINT

I want to share something that I've learned over 30 years in the insurance and financial services business. I've discovered that you must constantly ask yourself two questions: "Where am I?" and "How did I get here?" Answering these two questions is crucial if you are going to progress into the future!

In any business, some days are up, and some days are down. There are times when you just scratch your head and wonder what's going on in this world, and there are days when you're popping champagne and clinking long-stemmed Tiffany crystal glasses. But also, there are some days when you're surprised by the problems you face. I remember someone saying, "I feel like one of General Custer's men. I thought we were going out for a little ride, but when I looked up, we were surrounded and arrows were flying everywhere!"

As the insurance and financial services business continues to evolve, distribution of products has now reached a point where everyone in the industry needs to ask themselves these two questions every day. Why are these questions so important today? Because the model we have used for the past 10, 20, 30, or even

50 years has changed. We've hit the *inflection point*—that moment in time when the existing model no longer works. Is this only because of advances in technology? No. Has technology sped up the process? Yes. The change is certainly related to technology, but it's more profound than that. The fundamental change is that today, *customers are now in control.* They choose *when* they want to buy, *how* they want to buy, and *what* they want to buy. They have more options than ever, and in the future, they'll have even more options for service and products.

When I started in the insurance business more than three decades ago, I was a young man of just 21. I've seen a lot of change in our industry during my career, but I've also seen a lot remain the same. For years, carriers, companies, and agency firms rested on their laurels. With no real reason to change, processes and procedures often remained at the status quo. However, an important shift has occurred. Over the past decade, we have seen real change in the way our industry applies the latest technologies to its marketing and delivery systems. One fact is evident: the world is not showing any signs of slowing down. As technologies continue to evolve, so will the way our customers expect to do business.

Another major shift has occurred in our industry regarding customer involvement. Only a few years ago, the carrier/company controlled the parameters that determined how customers purchased. In the past, customers' choices were limited. Some made the observation, "It's like dressing a toddler: parents don't give a wide range of options. They just ask, 'Do you want this one or that one?'" As an industry, we didn't provide many variations in what was available, and customers had little control over their purchasing.

Today, it's more like dressing a teenager: the options are seemingly endless! Now, customers control the purchasing process. As they examine an array of options, they have access to more information, more choices, and more industry channels . . . with more options being added all the time. Today's customers are more informed. They not only desire, they *demand* a competent, specialized advisor to assist them. In today's world of information overload, our customers are looking for someone to guide them through the unknown—what I call "the maze of madness." They're not looking for someone to repeat the information they can find on their own. They're looking for a trusted advisor to help them avoid costly mistakes.

YOU CAN'T AFFORD TO WAIT

Who needs to respond to this challenge and these opportunities? All of us. When is the best time to get on the new wave of change? Yesterday . . . or at least now.

If you're on a team in an office, you're often the touch point for customers, so you need to understand that they need you far less for basic services because they can get them online. So, your role is changing. You need to go above and beyond the historical approach of team members by giving people more information and better service than they can get online.

If you're a broker/agent, you undoubtedly sense that the ground under your feet has already shifted. You know you've come to the inflection point in your business, so you're highly motivated to make the necessary changes to keep your business viable and profitable.

If you're a carrier executive, it's your task to equip every person who reports to you, in your office and in the field, to get in front of the new wave of change so they aren't swept away or left behind. It's your privilege to be a change agent to equip your people to take advantage of the changes that are already happening. Don't wait too long!

THRIVING THROUGH SPECIALIZATION

In this changing environment, we need to position ourselves and our firms to thrive. Although theoretically we can't be all things to all people, we want our customers to see us as supremely competent. This requires every person in our firm to be knowledgeable, professional, and informed, and it demands a level of specialization for every product and service we offer or recommend.

Specialization isn't a new concept for anyone who has heard me speak or has read any of my books, but specialization has evolved since we introduced the concept more than a decade ago. Actually, the fundamental concept hasn't changed, but the internal organization has. Not only does each team need to be specialized; we also need to create relationships with outside "specialized expertise partners" so we can immediately offer a wide range of high quality products and services to our customers.

We have to be prepared to offer our customers every product and service they desire, even when it's not in our product wheelhouse. This means knowing when we can take a service or coverage outside our firm and who to take it to. The connection and the process need to be seamless—customers must feel that they didn't leave your carrier or firm's ecosystem. And it requires a network of vetted providers. Together, we can create an attractive and workable relational network of multiple firms working together to meet our customers' needs.

Take a hard look at your role, firm, or carrier as it is today, and ask yourself, "Where am I now?" and "How did I get here?" Take a rigorously honest approach when looking at your business. What have you done right, and what could have been done better? Are you poised for the future? What areas could you improve? In what areas do you thrive? When is the last time you retooled any of your procedures or workflows? Many professionals show up every day without a real plan, and their schedules are dictated by the brushfires that flare up during the day. They don't have a defined and purposeful schedule to guide them.

Don't let that be you! Start today setting up your firm for success. Create an action plan to retool everyone and everything within your agency or firm.

The bottom line is to have a seamless ecosystem at the firm level and/or the carrier level. Think of it like a digital experience. You enter through the main hub, and when you are offered a different product, most of the time you feel you've left the hub. It feels odd and uncomfortable because the process has suddenly become complicated. Our task is to create a reality for our customers in which they never feel they've left our hub.

Let me stress the point again: To ride the new wave in our culture and our industry, you need to create a network that blends excellent customer experience, a wide array of options in your offerings, and the creation of expertise partners to whom you can refer your customers who need products and services you don't currently offer.

Learning to ride this wave takes creativity and tenacity, but you have it in you to learn, grow, and succeed in the new world of insurance and financial services.

The agencies, carriers, firms, agents, and team members who survive and thrive will be those that find, adapt to, and embrace the opportunities that surface during times of rapid change. That's what this book is about. I encourage you to read it through and mark the most important points for you. Have the people on your team read it, and take time to discuss how you'll implement changes. This book isn't a novel; it's a blueprint for a new business model.

CHAPTER 1
ADAPT OR DIE

Within every threat to the local agency's existence lies an opportunity to retool and capture more business than ever.

And the threats are very real. Do you remember when Walmart started taking over the world and opening up big-box stores in small communities? The retail behemoth put many small mom and pop appliance stores and other shops out of business.

In 2010, researchers at the University of Illinois at Chicago and Loyola University-Chicago found that stores within a four-mile radius of Walmart stores in the area of Chicago were more likely to go out of business than stores in other parts of the community.[1] The opening of Walmart stores caused nearly 100 businesses to close after its opening and eliminated the equivalent of about 300 full-time jobs—about as many jobs as the stores initially added to the area.

The Walmart stores, run well and efficiently, became the juggernauts that gobbled up all competitors. With good reason, many feared that soon, Walmart would be the only retail business left in America. The only way for local companies to survive was to adapt.

Amazon's growth mirrors the Walmart dynamic. In an article for *Entrepreneur*, A. J. Agrawal describes the impact of "the Amazon Effect": "By mid-2018, Amazon was already responsible for roughly 50 percent of the nation's ecommerce sales and 5 percent of all combined offline and online sales." The article states that some companies have adapted so they could survive: "Studies show that Amazon's success has led to some business closures, but many companies, in fact, have tackled the Amazon effect creatively and effectively to compete for customers and hold their ground. In short, the Amazon Effect is just another reason the retail environment is always in flux.[2]

THE WALMART/AMAZON EFFECT THREATENS OUR AGENCIES

Today, a similar situation is happening to the local insurance-agency storefronts in our local communities.

A 2018 Accenture report revealed that the personal distribution network is shrinking. The number of active insurance agents and brokers has declined to less than one-third of what it was 20 years ago. For those who remain, profitability is lagging.[3]

Ernst & Young's Insurance Outlook 2019 indicates that falling profitability for property & casualty (P&C) insurers in North and South America is the result of higher underwriting losses and a weak pricing environment in commercial lines. The report's authors state that nonlife insurers need to operate differently in the future. One suggestion, they say, is "strengthening direct channels to gradually reduce dependency on agents and brokers, particularly in personal and small commercial lines."[4] Through information I've gleaned in my consulting work with carriers in the areas of agent economics, I've found that this is an important way to adjust to market changes. However, this suggestion is unsettling—it means that the very survival of our businesses might depend on reducing the number of agents and brokers.

Despite their reach, the Walmarts, Amazons, and Costcos of the world don't have *all* the business. There are still local businesses—appliance stores, hardware stores, bookstores, auto-repair shops, and other service providers—that customize their services and know every customer's needs and preferences. Even in big cities, we can find pockets of local businesses that have loyal customers. They thrive because they have adapted to the consumer-controlled marketplace. They give their customers exactly what they want.

The owners of mom and pop stores that survived the relentless competition from Walmart did so by thinking differently than ever before. Some of them formed buying groups, and others began offering innovative value-added services and products they didn't previously offer.

They adapted to survive, and we need to follow their example today in the insurance and financial services industry.

WE MUST ADAPT TO SURVIVE

I want to share something critically important to every carrier, agent, team member, broker, firm, and company leader who will listen. The local presence, whether an exclusive agency, independent broker, or company-operated storefront, must adapt to a new model. The old model simply won't work any longer. Period. No questions. Drop the mic. It's done. You need to retool the way you deliver service and sales locally, or you'll soon be extinct.

But the real threat isn't technology, as many believe. The threat is *a failure to adapt to the new realities of the consumer marketplace.*

This isn't a new threat. Over the past few years, we've had plenty of notice that our survival depends on our ability to adapt to changes in the marketplace. Back in 2013, a McKinsey report stated,

> There are signs . . . that the economics of the traditional agent model are beginning to unravel. Where agents once served as the front line in risk selection and pricing, advances in predictive models are making this role obsolete. The agent was once the face of the insurance brand; now, customers increasingly use multiple channels to connect with their carrier. Perhaps most disruptive to the traditional agent value model, auto insurance—which accounts for 70 percent of personal lines premiums—is fast becoming commoditized.[5]

WE MUST LEVERAGE TECHNOLOGY, NOT FEAR IT

Granted, technology poses a threat to our personal distribution network as we've known it. Increasingly, people are using digital channels to purchase their auto insurance, as well as some property, business, and life insurance. But within this threat also lies a potential solution. Local agents need to leverage technology instead of fearing it.

A December 2018 report by McKinsey describes how technology is the catalyst for growth. It states, "Digital technologies are giving rise to ecosystems that could allow insurers to extend their reach or to partner with companies in other industries.

Carriers have an opportunity to differentiate themselves by providing an excellent customer experience across multiple points of contact."

For the P&C industry, the McKinsey researchers say that digitizing the claims function holds tremendous potential: "To capture the value of digital, P&C claims functions must embark on a transformation to become a customer-centric, digitally enabled organization that excels in the three foundational areas of claims: customer experience, efficiency, and effectiveness."[6]

No matter what role you play—from carrier executives to local team members—what you don't know *can* hurt you. Stay abreast of the latest industry developments and technology. The information you discover will empower you to keep growing.

RELY ON THE CLOUD TO STREAMLINE AGENCY FUNCTIONS

The obvious way to accomplish digitization of existing functions is to rely on *cloud* computing. That simply means that you store and access data and programs on the Internet instead of on a local device, such as your computer's hard drive.

One example of cloud-based computing is Dropbox, an application that allows you to store and share documents with others—even large documents you cannot send via email.

Using the cloud will streamline your processes, speed up your daily functions, improve communication among your team members, save money on software and servers, and enhance your efficiency, flexibility, collaboration efforts, and scalability. You no longer have to pay someone to regularly back up your data. Your data are safe and always available in the cloud.

Here's an example of how the cloud can save any small business time and money: Just about everyone uses the Microsoft Office suite of applications—Word, Excel, PowerPoint, and Access. Not too long ago, when you purchased a new computer, it already had the Microsoft Office suite already installed, or you had to buy the MS Office software separately, insert a disc into the computer, and install it on your new computer. Then, as Microsoft kept updating its software, you had to go through the cumbersome process of installing the new software manually. Many consumers concluded that Office and other software programs were obsolete as soon as they installed them.

But now you can simply purchase a subscription to Office 365 and other programs. This means you don't have to download and store the program on your computer—which saves you time and storage space. Also, when a company updates its software, your subscription gives you access to the latest version. No reinstallation is necessary. Plus, you can access those applications from anywhere—you don't have to be on your computer at the office to access them.

With every process and function you entrust to the cloud instead of handling it manually, you gain efficiency.

Ovum, a technology research firm, found via a survey that insurers are already leveraging cloud applications for core operational activities, although there is still plenty of room for growth here. The number of US insurers with claims systems fully deployed in the cloud increased from 13 percent in Ovum's 2016 survey to 26 percent in 2018.[7]

Moving your primary business functions to the cloud requires planning. Develop a cloud strategy as a multiyear, phased migration process. You'll need to hire an employee or find a consultant to upgrade processes and resources to achieve your cloud strategy. You'll also need to identify the applications and workloads that will be migrated to the cloud and develop security policies to protect them.

In the end, technology is just a tool we use to get things done more quickly and easily. Keep in mind that many consumers research their options online, but they still value our expertise in helping them make purchases.

According to the 2018 Insurance Barometer Study survey by the Life and Health Insurance Foundation for Education (LIFE) and LIMRA, even though 45 percent of consumers of all ages say they would go online to find more information about life insurance, they prefer to complete the purchase with an agent or financial advisor.[8]

PRACTICAL WAYS TO USE THE CLOUD

Knowing that consumers are in control today and that they value the advice we can give them, how can we leverage technology? Here are five ways to leverage cloud technology to meet the needs of today's in-control customers. (Some of these solutions require upper level carrier resources, but others can be implemented on a local level.)

1. Work with the appropriate tech specialist to build an app that provides 24/7 solutions to customers' needs.

Customers are now accustomed to the Amazon standard of on-demand access to every purchasing option. Build an app that meets this expectation. If you already have an app but it's been a while since you tweaked it, study your stats. Talk with some customers who use the app to find out what they like and what could be improved.

2. Make it easy for customers to file claims online.

In 2014, Suncorp Group Limited transformed its insurance claims assessment process. The company digitized its claim form and made it available online. Then it went one step further and automated the process, using IBM Watson to analyze the details associated with each claim and to assess liability. The outcome was so positive that Suncorp now processes half of all its claims using this "zero-touch" methodology.[9]

3. Streamline and personalize your marketing communications.

Again, you can benefit from leveraging the cloud in this area. For example, Maropost Marketing Cloud can help you automate your marketing communications and target leads more precisely.

4. Respond to customers more quickly.

Today, customers want to get their questions answered and buy products 24/7/365, and the cloud makes this possible. Employees in any location who have Internet access can respond to customers at any time of the day.

5. Make better use of your valuable data.

Although our industry is a little slower than others in adapting to cloud storage, we get high marks for capturing data. Through the past century, data have been the backbone of our business. Case in point: actuarial tables. However, we don't always optimize the potential of our data. The cloud helps us capture data about our customers, store it, safeguard it, and analyze it for optimum planning.

Artificial intelligence (AI) tools are constantly improving data management. For example, these tools can monitor online searches and transactions and then personalize customers' experiences on your website or app.

The 2019 "State of the Connected Consumer" report from Salesforce reports that 67 percent of customers expect companies to provide new products and services more frequently than before. Also, 75 percent of customers expect companies to use new technologies to improve their experiences, and 62 percent are open to the use of AI to improve their experiences—up from 59 percent in 2018. These consumers are making the most of today's technology—76 percent of the respondents say they use a connected device, and 29 percent have a smart speaker in their home.[10]

Capturing data is just the first step—we then have to make sense of it. That's difficult to do because of the massive volumes of data being generated through social media, company transactions, wearable sensors, telematics, and other sources. This is an area all of us, including underwriters, need to consider a priority. Kate Browne, Underwriters Counsel at Swiss Re Corporate Solutions, says, "The underwriter of the future will be able to unlock the power of data and analytics to aggressively price the best risks, avoid the poor ones, and support growth."[11]

EVOLVE TO IOT AND AI

At the very least, we need to connect systems across the insurance value chain—particularly claims and policy administration.[12]

From there, we need to eventually evolve to leveraging powerful technologies such as the Internet of Things (IoT) to use real-time data to reduce or eliminate claims and artificial intelligence to streamline claims management. By consolidating our operations, we will enhance customer service and shorten response times while improving service quality, data management, and financial reporting. Many of the advances in new technology need to be produced by carriers, with training and implementation on the local level.

IoT refers to a vast number of gadgets that connect to the Internet to share data with other gadgets. Internet-connected devices have sensors built into them to collect data and use those data to make our lives easier. An example of this technology is the "smart refrigerator." LG's InstaView Smart refrigerator has a transparent front panel that allows owners to see what's inside the main fridge section without opening the door.

In our industry, an example of IoT is wearable sensors that monitor people's vital signs. Wearables are so commonplace at John Hancock that they lower premiums in 100 percent of the company's life insurance policies. Another IoT-related technology is drones. These unmanned devices can move into disaster zones within minutes and capture accurate data for property claims. During the 2018 natural disasters in the southeastern United States, a company called Geomni provided claims support to four of the top ten property & casualty insurers.[13]

Many of us in this industry don't even know where to begin to modernize our core systems and digitize our operations. The key is to look to the experts in this field. We excel in our own areas but not every area, so it makes sense to enlist the assistance of people who are experts in this type of work. One such company is Infosys, which specializes in next-generation digital services and consulting in 45 countries. In 2019, Infosys surveyed 187 executives from financial services and insurance organizations with more than $1 billion in revenues across the United States, Europe, Australia, and New Zealand.[14]

Infosys found that although our industry recognizes that digital transformation will lead to enhanced agility, scalability, and efficiency—and therefore increased customer satisfaction—many in our industry are apprehensive about data security and regulatory compliance. However, the increasing sophistication of cybersecurity measures is gradually enticing our industry to consider the public cloud more willingly.

The Infosys study revealed the top three drivers that ranked high among US companies that are adopting cloud services: the opportunities offered by evolving customer needs, emerging technologies, and competition.[15]

Here is a note of caution: don't focus on technological advances so much that you forget your unique value as a caring, empathetic, knowledgeable human being. As trusted advisors, we add a human element that's quickly becoming extinct in the insurance and financial services industry. We can't afford to lose our personal touch!

CHAPTER 2
IF YOU CAN'T BEAT 'EM . . .

When technology, demographics, or the marketplace disrupts business as we know it, it's easy to panic. Instead, we need to analyze every apparent setback and discover how we can turn each one into an opportunity.

CASE IN POINT: KOHL'S STORES NOW ACCEPT AMAZON RETURNS

When retailing giant Kohl's began experiencing sagging sales in 2017, the company didn't just throw in the towel and complain that Amazon was putting the company out of business. Instead, Kohl's launched a pilot program to begin accepting Amazon.com returns at its stores in Chicago and Los Angeles.[16] The pilot program performed particularly well, leading to 9 percent growth in new customers and 8 percent growth in revenues in those cities, compared with national growth of 1 percent and 2 percent, respectively, according to payment data analyzed by Earnest Research.[17]

In July 2019, Kohl's expanded its Amazon returns program nationwide. If you're a customer, you don't need a shipping box for your returned item. Just log on to your Amazon.com account, click on the box that says you want to return the item, and show the QR code you received to the Kohl's customer service rep. They're hoping that while you're there, you'll browse . . . and buy. In fact, when you return an Amazon item at Kohl's, you receive a coupon for a 25 percent discount on any Kohl's purchase, and you can use the coupon immediately.

Instead of succumbing to the Amazon juggernaut, Kohl's found a way to ride the shirttails of the giant. Ten years ago, Kohl's leadership probably would never have imagined that accepting Amazon returns would one day be their biggest and brightest idea.

Kohl's began accepting Amazon returns at all 1,150 of its stores in July 2019. Just three weeks later, foot traffic in Kohl's stores increased nearly 24 percent, according to location-data advertising firm inMarket.[18]

We have no way of knowing if this approach will continue to be successful. But for now, it's a shining example of how to adapt to and benefit from change—even if the change appears to be detrimental at first glance.

This type of innovation is apparent in other industries as well. Some banks have opened coffee houses inside their doors, with space for people to work. This unexpected approach gives people a sense of community and builds loyalty to their brand. Customers appreciate the comfort and convenience, even though it isn't directly related to the primary service banks normally offer.

For every type of business, including insurance agencies, storefront economics have changed. The old model is no longer sufficient to serve customers who are digitally inclined and willing to think far beyond the way we've always done things.

Remember, we are now at the inflection point—that moment in time when the existing model no longer works.

OUR MARGIN ON AUTO COVERAGE IS NO LONGER ENOUGH

Because customer expectations have evolved so much, we can no longer rely on our auto-coverage margin to sustain our agencies. We need to shuffle the deck. I have been conducting studies and sharing my findings on this subject for the past five years. The indications we saw five years ago have become a reality.

In April 2019, J.D. Power reported that auto insurance revenue hit $245 billion in 2018, reflecting industrywide growth of 6.2 percent. But 54 percent of those gains ($7.8 billion in direct-written premium) came from only two companies: Progressive Insurance and GEICO — two leaders in the direct-to-consumer space. This means an increasing amount of auto insurance is being sold directly from manufacturers to consumers, with no agent involvement. Authors of the report stated, "The shift in consumer behavior in the auto insurance industry is quickly moving from face-to-face to digital as large, well-capitalized insurers give consumers the tools to shop as they would for any other consumer product. Increasingly, those insurers who get that consumer model right are the ones who will dominate the market."[19]

To compete with these direct-to-consumer leaders, carriers are cutting expenses, and one of the biggest expenses is distribution. Personal distribution must support the cost of employee salaries, wages, and benefits. With increased competition and decreased market share, carriers feel pressure to reduce commissions, yet they still want their exclusive and independent agents to deliver unrivaled service.

But it's just not good business to reduce agents' commissions while asking them to provide a higher level of service. Our most compelling value as trusted advisers is getting to know every customer and tailoring solutions to his or her changing protection needs. Robo-advisors will never be able to compete with personal advisors on this value point.

To provide exemplary service, agents need the support of their carriers. Independent agents lack this support in many cases. The J.D. Power 2019 US Independent Insurance Agent Satisfaction StudySM revealed that the satisfaction level of agents regarding the service their insurers provide them is among the lowest of business relationships that J.D. Power measures. Independent agents who are satisfied with the service their insurers provide them are more likely to recommend that carrier and place a greater number of products with that insurer. The report notes that the most important factors that determine agent satisfaction are support and communication in personal lines and quoting in commercial lines.[20] Carriers need to pay attention to the strong correlation between independent agents' satisfaction and placement rate.

Carriers need to encourage their agents to fully embrace their role as trusted advisors to their clients and meet their unique needs. The agents who thrive are those who provide tailored solutions and excel at multichannel marketing, while increasing their scale and operational efficiency." (I wrote in great detail on this subject in my book, *Discussion Partner*.)

USE AUTO COVERAGE AS THE FOUNDATION FOR OTHER SALES— CREATE THE 360-DEGREE VIEW

It's a sobering fact that we can no longer live on auto coverage alone. But the great news is that auto coverage is still the pressing consumer need that will open doors to bigger and better opportunities.

We predicted this trend about ten years ago. We saw that auto insurance leads to business insurance, life insurance, and financial-only services—the total 360-degree view of the customer. Instead of depending on auto insurance as a profit-making engine, we began viewing it as a launching pad to other coverages. I still believe that's the path forward.

Local agents need to view themselves as the Walmarts or Amazons of the protection marketplace. We need to offer everything consumers will ever need. If we don't get out in front of this, we risk being gobbled up by robo-advisors and monolithic financial services companies. We need to operate within extended and effective ecosystems that give us and our consumers access to every possible product and service.

We need to continue to sell auto insurance and collaborate with those who provide other offerings. You can be the carrier or firm that has a network of well-educated advisors and great depth. But every time you leave a potential service or sale uninvestigated, someone else will move in and take it. It's crucial to offer advice and product options on everything our industry has to offer. I predict that local agencies and firms that fail to heed this warning will be on their way out of business in less than two years. For this reason alone, we must retool and change the way we have always done business in the past.

If this sounds disturbing, it is. My goal is to disturb you into the realization that you need to offer everything, or you will eventually offer nothing. This is further proof that the customer is in control. We will thrive only by meeting our customers' ever-evolving needs.

TWO EXAMPLES OF RETOOLING IN OUR INDUSTRY

In the past, there was a fine line of demarcation between property & casualty companies and financial services firms. But now, in an effort to offer more products and services to more customers, the line between the two types of companies is becoming blurred by mergers and acquisitions. Let me describe a couple of examples.

1. State Farm now offers financial planning.

Toward the end of 2018, State Farm, the largest property, casualty, and auto insurance provider in the nation, began asking its agents to pass the Series 65 exam by the end of 2019.[21] They had to pass the exam to become licensed investment adviser representatives. Now, instead of describing just insurance on its website, State Farm gives equal emphasis to insurance and investments.[22]

2. AXA Is Getting into the P&C Business.

In 2018, upon its $15.3 billion cash acquisition of XL Group, AXA created a new division called AXA XL that is dedicated to large property & casualty commercial lines and specialty risks. AXA XL combined XL Group operations, AXA Corporate Solutions, and AXA Art and is operating under the master brand of AXA.[23]

The perceived downside of this merger is that, in early 2019, some people lost their jobs. As the company began transferring employees to one company, AXA announced that it was going to cut 711 positions in Europe. That represents 7.5 percent of AXA XL's global workforce.[24]

Ideally, we want to retool our companies and agencies without a loss of jobs or a loss of representation to the people in our communities, but these large-scale corporate shifts demonstrate that this is no longer business as usual. This is a prime example of the inflection point—the moment in time when the existing model no longer works and we need to find a more effective one.

HOW TO RETOOL YOUR AGENCY MODEL

Now that you know what's at stake, let's look at solutions. Thought leader Jim Rohn used to say, "I'm waiting for somebody to come give me the plan, but what if they never show up?"

Well, I'm developing a plan. Currently, I'm working with several carriers and firms to build an open-platform solution to help their advisors get a 360-degree view of customers so they can offer every option in insurance and financial services. But for now, here are some easily implementable strategies to help you adapt and retool your agency model.

1. Assess where you are now and where you want to be.

The first step is to assess where you are. Then do a gap analysis to determine how you can get from where you are now to where you want to be. You can download templates online to help you perform a gap analysis on sites like Smartsheet, iAuditor, and ClearPoint Analysis.

Analytics matter, and your projections must be based on reality. Where is your cash flow coming from? What are the demographics of your client base? What do you need to do to turn your model upside down without disrupting your current cash flow or your existing customer base? And how can you do this in a seamless way, so your customers don't even realize that you have retooled? For example, is it possible that your agency/firm or carrier needs to become a service organization that sells protection products instead of being a sales organization that provides service? The key is to change the back room and leave the front room the way it is.

2. Get a 360-degree view of your customers.

Your overall objective, whether you're a company executive, carrier, agency owner, broker, or team member, is to get a 360-degree view of all your potential and existing customers.

What do they need? How are those needs changing? How can you meet those needs, through your own offerings and through collaboration with other experts in your direct market area? Study your customers, and improve your knowledge, your skills, and your content.

Gather data, and then study those numbers to get meaningful insights. If you don't have someone on your team who excels in this area, hire a firm that does. Data are meaningless unless you figure out what the numbers mean.

3. Be willing to offer free advice, even to people who aren't clients.

Instead of just being a quote-giver, be a trusted advisor—or what I call a Discussion Partner. Clearly explain to prospects and customers how one product differs from another, even if your product may not be the best product. Maybe one product provides coverage that the other product doesn't, or one company pays claims in a way more advantageous to the customer. Sometimes the customer may not be looking for all the bells and whistles a product or company offers, but instead just wants a simple policy to protect them from being sued, and that is perfectly acceptable as well as long as you educate them on their options.

4. Be transparent.

Tell your prospects and clients the good, the bad, and the ugly of all of it.

If you are an executive or captive agent, say, "I need to disclose to you that I'm a preferred agent with this company. I get a commission, and in some cases, I get bonuses for the volume I sell." But then give prospects and clients the good news—that through your partnerships and collaborations, you can get them any product or service they want. You may even tell them, "I want you to have the best coverage possible, and I don't think our product is the ideal one for you. I recommend that you go with this other product. I won't get a commission on it, but my goal is to make sure you have the best coverage possible. Let's schedule a video conference with my partner over at XYZ who specializes in this coverage." This is a great way to build trust with your clients while expanding your offerings.

5. Think innovatively.

We saw that Kohl's is keeping afloat because it's accepting Amazon returns. That's the kind of innovation that helps companies adapt and thrive. Brainstorm with your team and with other bright people you know. What can you do differently that will add value to what you do and showcase the unique value you've always offered and will continue to offer?

6. Stay in business because your community needs you.

I know people who have been insurance agents for decades, and they're dropping out. They don't want to retool, and they don't know how to adapt—but their communities need them, and 20 or so employees depend on those agencies for their income. Your employees shop in your local restaurants, grocery stores, and oil-change shops. They make good money, and they support your local economy. Your employees and your community need your agency to stay open, but they also need you to stay involved by participating in charitable works to care for people in need. This activism extends your ability to make a difference far beyond the walls of your office.

ADVICE TO CARRIERS, COMPANIES, AND AGENTS

The responsibility for changing the structure of our industry begins with carriers and companies and their distribution. Here are some suggestions for leading the charge to adapt.

1. Encourage collaboration at all levels.

Help your distribution—whether independent, exclusive, employee-led, or contractor-led—see the bigger picture. Train, teach, and develop them to be Discussion Partners to their customers and offer access to everything they need. Again, this typically requires establishing partnerships and collaborations with other local experts who offer products and services you don't offer. Expand your network so you can expand your service.

Expand your customers' access to all services through relationships, strategic alliances, partnerships, distribution, and agreements with other companies, carriers, and providers of information. This is actually easy to do, and the results will benefit everyone involved. Identify niche areas of service that are unique to your geographical area, and find out which reps are known locally for being experts in those areas. Reach out to them, and find out how you can collaborate in mutually beneficial ways. Chances are, you and your team have expertise in areas that other reps don't, and vice versa. Working together, you can collectively serve more clients with unrivaled service. In this way, everyone wins.

It's critical that those of us who lead local agencies and firms do everything in our power to show customers that we are their solution for every possible need. We need to educate our consumers about the value of every product and solution. More importantly, we need to offer global answers locally, working within a carefully constructed large-scale ecosystem.

For example, anyone who has ever had a family member endure a long-term illness can relate to the need for long-term care insurance. Explain to your customers how important it is to be prepared. And if they say, "Well, it's expensive," tell them the truth: "It might be, but it won't be as expensive as losing your income, your house, and everything else you own after you add up all the medical expenses." Tell them that even if they don't buy the coverage from you, you want them to be protected. The same thing goes for umbrella insurance, life insurance, short- and long-term disability insurance, crop insurance for farmers, data insurance for companies, and every other product and service.

When discussing our customers' needs, we need to keep in mind that personal risk management and business risk management must include the option of non-insurance products. Sometimes a client self-insures. For instance, let's say a couple owns a farm or a large piece of timbered property. They might have a pole barn for horses or some other kind of structure that appears to be uninsurable, or in their minds, they don't consider it to be worth insuring. They acknowledge the risk and choose to not buy coverage. By getting to know your customers and building trusted relationships with them, you will learn about their unique needs and find the right coverage for them.

Similarly, some people don't need any of the life insurance products we provide because they use their old policies or other insurance products for this need. Some may even set aside cash or create "a sinking fund."

We could list many other examples, but here's the bottom line: gifted and valued advisors (Discussion Partners) talk about every available resource—not just what they're selling and not limited to insurance products. Instead, they look at consumers' needs from every angle.

In one form or another, local advisors must be the gateway to all answers, solutions, content, and delivery of products. Leave no stone unturned. Offer customers every possible option in one place . . . or someone else will.

2. Reconsider the exclusive-agent model.

According to the J.D. Power 2019 U.S. Insurance Shopping Study cited earlier, success in acquiring new customers depends on having a strong brand and meeting customer expectations of convenience and competitive pricing. When it comes to these important traits, J.D. Power says direct and independent agents are best positioned, while insurers that are largely reliant on exclusive agents for new business growth are facing headwinds.

The study notes that direct and independent agent models resonate with customers and continue to show increasingly higher levels of customer satisfaction, while the exclusive agent channel is falling behind. Tom Super, vice president of Insurance Intelligence at J.D. Power, observed, "We're entering a new era of consumerism in the auto insurance marketplace, in which customers are in the driver's seat when it comes to the shopping and servicing of their policies." He added that today's customers value choice, personalization, and a strong reputation in their insurance shopping. "That puts significant pressure on insurers to get their customer models just right, with the proper mix of self-service tools, strong brand awareness and an engaged distribution network."[25]

I believe the existing exclusive agent model is in a perfect position to be overhauled and reconfigured.

We're not in a sales world anymore; we're in a service-first, information, and content world. The days are long gone of simply giving quotes and saying, "Here's your price. Do you want it?" That won't work in the future (or the present). Why invest an hour of your time to give someone a quote if you're not going to get to know that person and form a deeper relationship?

If you and your team aren't currently equipped to become your customers' one-stop shop, please acquire the knowledge and skills to do so. The survival of your firm, your team members' jobs, and your valuable contributions to your local community depend on it.

CHAPTER 3

WHAT CUSTOMERS WANT

Today, the customer is in control.

There was a time when tradition and longevity in the market were hallmarks of success in the insurance industry, and carriers had complete control over every step of the purchasing cycle. But today, agility, innovation, and transparency are the characteristics of market leaders. These traits enable companies to thrive as our business is evolving due to rapid advancements in technology and other factors.

Gone are the days of carriers leading the entire purchasing cycle of insurance products and financial services. Today, customers lead the way, and technology makes it easy for them to purchase virtually any product and access any service. With a few clicks of a mouse, people can order groceries, prescriptions, take-out meals, and even new cars. They can even deposit checks from their phones. And again, the Amazon Effect gives shoppers instant product comparisons, user reviews, recommendations, expedited shipping, and other features they now expect as standard service.

Given this significant shift toward customer control, our industry is moving toward total transparency in coverages and pricing. Customers will know all the details when they purchase property & casualty products, financial services products, life insurance products, and more, in much the same way financial services and securities are sold today.

THE MOVE TOWARD TOTAL TRANSPARENCY REQUIRES A DIFFERENT APPROACH

This drastic change is a bit scary because carriers (and captive agents) haven't had to deal with this type of consumer landscape before, although brokers have had comp raters for a long time.

The solution is logical and simple.

To transition smoothly into the customer-driven sales cycle, all of us—from carrier executives to agents and team members—need to differentiate ourselves by *identifying a strong value proposition* and *communicating it consistently* across all platforms. Even if you aren't the lowest-cost option, you shouldn't be afraid to be compared to competitors because price isn't everything. When you have sufficiently differentiated your unique product and service offerings and have configured your offers for your ideal customers, you will no longer have to focus on (and worry about) competing on price.

After you *define* and *communicate* the unique value proposition of your product and distribution ecosystem, lead with this unique attribute. Communicate it relentlessly through all levels of your organization. New technology, strategic partnerships, improved service, and faster claims processing will never help you gain traction if your employees have no idea what their value proposition is to the customers.

Defining your unique value proposition is much easier when you have a 360-degree view of the consumer and when the consumer has a 360-degree view of your offerings.

INTRODUCING OPEN PLATFORM SOLUTION (OPS)

Open Platform Solution (OPS) enables customers, as well as agents and advisors, to get a complete 360-degree view of all available coverages and costs. I'm working with other thought leaders, technology companies, consulting firms, vendors, and carriers to create a middleware platform to help customers find the right protection and financial products for their needs. This platform will simplify the customer experience, enhance customers' visibility of insurance product offerings, and create growth opportunities for advisors and carriers alike.

OPS is an insurance and financial institution's ability to offer a 360-degree view of available products and services, both proprietary and external. It's simply an acknowledgment that no one agent, carrier, representative (independent or exclusive), or broker can be all things to all people. Instead, with a 360-degree view of product solutions, we can have a discussion about what is best for each client, regardless of the commissions involved—even if they aren't our own company's proprietary products.

I firmly believe that property & casualty protection will move rapidly to a complete 360-degree view. This view will allow us to discuss the ideal option for each individual, family, and business owner for P&C coverage, life insurance, financial services, and other related services.

BUILD YOUR VALUE PROPOSITION AROUND CUSTOMERS' WANTS AND NEEDS

Carriers and their distribution need to continue to develop innovative new products and create new markets that are built around what customers want and have every right to expect. Every product that exists today, and new products that will enter the marketplace, must have a clear and concise value proposition. Every team member within the carrier and its distribution should be in lockstep with that value proposition.

What's your value proposition? What sets your products and services apart from others? Define a value proposition that's compelling enough to attract and retain customers for the long term. Then communicate it to everyone in your organization— in as many different venues as possible and as often as possible. When asked, "What is your unique value proposition?" every team member should state your value proposition word for word . . . and without hesitation. If someone misses the mark, keep repeating it, and keep explaining why it's so important.

Let's look at two examples of value propositions that focus on what customers are responding to in today's business climate:

Value Proposition #1: "We blend a convenient, state-of-the-art digital platform with expert agent insight."

The information we provide our customers must be delivered by professional advisor teams, digital strategies, telephonic support, and any other available media support. Armed with the proper value proposition, a carrier/company can deliver its products and services through an ecosystem of distribution. This means a total commitment to digital, current technologies, future technologies, telephony, and most importantly, a local advisor or independent contractor to create a local powerhouse firm.

If the insurance industry embraces technology and part-ners with outstanding companies, we can provide a wider range services to our customers. For example, AXA is expanding its network of collaboration to work with two giants in the technol-ogy world: Apple and IBM. A site illustrating a number of Apple's "success stories" states: "Empowered with iPad Pro and a custom app developed with IBM, insurance sales advisors at AXA France now sit side by side with their customers to build a complete fi-nancial picture, allowing them to create collaborative, trusted relationships." And David Guillot De Suduiraut, CIO of AXA France explains, "We want to provide our customers with a sim-ple and engaging experience. Apple technology is helping us do that."[26] It seems there are no limits to the expansion of a seamless ecosystem.

Information is currency. This is true for Millennials (those born between 1980 and 1995) more than any other generation. Studies are in agreement that Millennials prefer to shop online, and they expect instant results. They have little patience with in-surance administration. For this reason, websites like Goodfetch let consumers compare prices for policies through various com-panies quickly and easily.[27]

One study reports that in 2019, Millennials made 60 per-cent of their purchases online, up from 47 percent in 2017. Also, Millennials now make 36 percent of their total purchases using mobile devices, up 20 percentage points from 2017.[28] However, it would be a mistake to assume that Millennials never want to in-teract with a human. According to the 2018 Insurance Barometer Study survey by the Life and Health Insurance Foundation for

Education (LIFE) and LIMRA, more than half of Millennials would research life insurance online, but they would purchase life insurance from a financial professional. Gen-Xers (those born between 1965 and 1980) are the group most likely (32 percent) to research and complete the purchase entirely online.[29]

Also, Millennial business owners are more likely than those in other generations to value the expertise an agent provides them. According to Nationwide's fourth annual Business Owner Survey, 69 percent of Millennial business owners work with an insurance agent, followed by Boomers at 66 percent and Gen X at 59 percent. The most common reason for working with an insurance agent among all generations is the trust that business owners place on the guidance and expertise from an agent.[30]

Carriers and companies can distinguish themselves by blending a highly interactive digital experience and quick response time with the expert advice and insight that only an experienced agent can provide.

Value Proposition #2: "We collect and process data in a meaningful way so we can provide you with more accurate and personalized premium models."

Without a doubt, the insurtech momentum is gaining at light speed. What is insurtech? The term "refers to the use of technology innovations designed to squeeze out savings and efficiency from the current insurance industry model. Insurtech is a combination of the words 'insurance' and 'technology,' inspired by the term fintech."

Our great industry has remained stagnant for some time, with incremental growth at best, in the property & casualty marketplace. Insurtech start-ups are exploring avenues that large insurance firms have less incentive to exploit, such as offering ultra-customized policies and using new streams of data from internet-enabled devices to price premiums according to observed behavior. Using input from all types of devices, including GPS tracking of cars to offer a more accurate and defined rate based on individual driving habits, these companies are building more finely delineated groupings of risk, allowing products to be priced more competitively.[31]

Although the initial response when outside influences begin gaining traction is to dig in our heels and fight them, many traditional insurance companies are discovering unique value in partnering with insurtechs to offer customers the best possible options. When we blend decades of experience in underwriting with innovative mechanisms for gathering data, we can customize policies and develop pricing that's tailored more to each customer's individual needs.

According to a 2019 McKinsey & Company report, digital networking via the Internet of Things (IoT) enables insurers to reduce costs and generate additional revenue. By harnessing data from devices that are equipped with sensors and automatic-activation functions, insurers can much more accurately assess risk with regard to issues like health habits and driving behaviors.[32]

Partnering with technology experts will enable you to offer more frequent and convenient customer interaction, optimize your resources, extend safety standards and reduce fraud, thus making it all about the customer.

BE A WINNER

I'm afraid far too many of us make colossal (and wrong) assumptions about our customers. We think we understand what
they're thinking and feeling, but our beliefs are based on the
model for our business 30 years ago.

We need to look beneath the surface into their lives to discover their current thoughts, feelings, hopes, and dreams. To
understand them more fully, we need to study the culture where
they live. Why are we so often wrong about the people we serve?
Maybe we're afraid we don't have what it takes to get below the
surface. Maybe we realize we're a couple of decades behind, and
it'll require a lot of time and effort for us to catch up. Or maybe
we're just on autopilot and don't want the stress of learning new
things. Whatever the reason, our job is to understand our customers so well that we can anticipate their needs. When we do
that, we can provide products and services to protect them and
help them be more successful.

Your unique value proposition obviously will be shaped by
your location, the demographics of your market, the products
you sell, and other factors. Whatever your unique offering is, define it, communicate it, and showcase it wherever possible.

Build your clients' confidence in you so they trust your advice on everything—not just on their insurance and financial
services moves, but on other life situations as well. And make it
a give-and-take conversation. Give them reassurance with your
expertise, but invite them to offer their input and information,
too. Encourage them to provide input, but assure them that you
will do the heavy lifting.

In the conclusion to its 2019 Insurance Industry Outlook, Deloitte states that the winners in the race to become the insurers of the future will likely be those who understand how to create competitive advantage in this new world. The report states, "A key element will likely be agility, determined by an insurer's ability to take advantage of new technology and data sets, design services and solutions rather than products and transform its operating platforms through collaborative initiatives and ecosystems in a pragmatic and material way."[33]

But let me offer a word of warning: quit waiting on the perfect technology. Find a workable system and use it. Yes, something better will come along almost before you get your people trained, but that's the nature of the modern world of business. Update when you need to, but not before you have to. If another company has something flashier, don't worry about it. It wasn't that long ago when we did everything on paper. Our recording and monitoring systems were cumbersome, but we made it work for the people we served.

Today, we have far better tools to capture and use information to serve our customers—even if our technology isn't the very latest on the market. The computer has changed our business, but it hasn't replaced the fundamental necessities of reading and writing, and spellcheck hasn't eliminated the need for us to carefully review our communication so it's clear, accurate, and professional. Technology can enhance our communication, but it can never take our place in our customers' lives.

I believe the opportunity for growth in the P&C industry has never been greater. The changes that are forcing our industry to step up and innovate are the same forces that will weed out the no-longer-relevant carrier providers.

CHAPTER 4

GETTING IT RIGHT

Merriam-Webster defines *experience* as "direct observation of or participation in events as a basis of knowledge." Experience is hands-on; it's learning, understanding, and acting on what we've discovered. Experience brings a subject matter to life, taking it from 2-D to 4-D. What we learn through experience sticks with us longer than what we merely read or hear about, and it has a greater chance of being forever etched into our memories.

In an article for *Fast Company*, Chip and Dan Heath observe, "Within any given span of experience, then, some moments will always be vastly more meaningful and memorable than others. As recipients of experiences, we understand this, but as creators of experiences, we ignore it . . . Moments matter. And our research suggests that people's most positive moments share certain traits in common, such as elevation, or being lifted out of the ordinary . . . If we understand what powerful moments are made of, we can be intentional about creating them. And the right moment can have extraordinary power."[34]

Experience is a necessary tool for all people to glean a deeper comprehension of any situation or subject matter. For this reason, we need to learn how to give unrivaled customer *service*, along with a memorable and meaningful customer *experience*. Anyone can be trained to answer a phone and take information from a customer. Anyone can be trained to mail out a birthday card, greet customers with a smile when they come through the front door, and give good customer service. But is this enough to retain the customers we have worked so hard to get? I think not.

STAND OUT FROM THE COMPETITION, WHATEVER IT TAKES

In June 2019, Salesforce released its third "State of the Connected Consumer" report. It revealed that 84 percent of customers say the *experience* a company provides is as important as its products or services. Also, 73 percent of customers expect companies to understand their needs and expectations, but 52 percent of customers say companies are generally impersonal.[35]

As our industry continues to transform and new purchasing platforms arise, we need to learn how to stand out from the competition. It's not just about selling products and services. It's about giving great service and selling yourself, your staff, and the company(ies) you represent to your clients. Why your agency/firm? Why your company/carrier? Why your suite of products and services? What makes you different than the ten other insurance and financial services offices the customers (or prospective customers) drove by on their way in to see you?

According to a *Forbes* article called "Customer Experience Is the New Brand," today, 89 percent of companies compete primarily on the basis of customer experience, up from just 36 percent in 2010. That's almost everyone! But company leaders think they are having more impact than they do. Although 80 percent of companies believe they deliver "super experiences," only 8 percent of customers agree.[36] That's a problem . . . a very big problem.

Everything a company or agency/firm does—marketing, research, advertising, and more—plays a role in shaping the customer experience. Focusing on customer experience management (CXM) may be the single most important investment a brand can make in today's competitive business climate.

It's time to get creative! You need to create positive customer experiences that will send you straight to the top of the pack. Thinking alone won't make it so. Good ideas need to be put into action to provide unrivaled service to every customer and potential customer you serve.

WE HAVE FEW CHANCES TO GET IT RIGHT

A 2018 PwC (PricewaterhouseCooper) study reveals that today's in-control customers walk away from brands and companies that fail to give them a positive customer experience. The report says that in the United States, even if people love your company or product, 59 percent will walk away after several bad experiences and 17 percent after just one bad experience. And if they don't love your company or product, 32 percent would stop doing business with an entire brand (not just stop buying a single product) they previously loved after just one bad experience.[37]

For this reason, it's imperative to provide unrivaled service and customer experiences. In fact, the PwC study says a positive customer experience is more valuable to attract and retain customers than advertising. Think about the billions of dollars the companies in our industry have spent on advertising in the past decades. Creating consistently great customer experiences is much more powerful than all that effort and expense!

Here are additional highlights from the PwC study that show the necessity of providing positive customer experience:

» Good customer experience leaves consumers feeling heard, seen, and appreciated. It has a tangible impact that can be measured in dollars and cents.

» 73 percent of all people point to customer experience as an important factor in their purchasing decisions, yet only 49 percent of U.S. consumers say companies provide a good customer experience today.

» 43 percent of all consumers would pay more for greater convenience, and 42 percent would pay more for a friendly, welcoming experience. Among U.S. customers, 65 percent find a positive experience with a brand to be more influential than great advertising.

» Nearly 80 percent of American consumers point to speed, convenience, knowledgeable help, and friendly service as the most important elements of a positive customer experience.

» Across all the industries surveyed, an average of 48 percent of U.S. consumers pointed to friendly, welcoming service as uniquely defining success in an industry, while only 32 percent pointed to having the most up-to-date technology.

There is no question that in today's customer-controlled marketplace, providing a positive customer experience is driving revenue. You can't afford *not to* create exceptional client experiences for everyone you serve.

SIX STRATEGIES

Let me offer six simple strategies you can implement immediately to enhance the customer experience in your own office. These are simple ideas that require minimal effort from you and your staff. They require only a simple shift in your daily routine, yet they can have an immediate, positive impact on your business.

1. Create, fine-tune, and tell your story.

Before you can demonstrate to your customers how and why you offer unrivaled service and experiences, you need to have a clear picture in your own mind.

Get your team together to write your group's story based on your value proposition, describing why and how your team offers memorable, meaningful experiences that customers appreciate. It can be as short as two or three sentences, and in fact, it will be more memorable if you keep it short and powerful. When you have all agreed on the story, have everyone practice it to ensure that everyone knows it by heart. This story should be personal to all of you—which includes how the story taps into each one's passion and purpose. There's a reason everyone on the team shows up every day at the same address: you believe in your business and what you're offering to your customers and your community. Convey this passion and commitment to your existing and potential customers. Your passion will translate into a deeper understanding of who you and your staff are. It will ensure higher customer retention, reduce attrition, and build deeper trust with your customers.

Knowing and sharing your compelling story will allow you to earn the right to place additional products and services into every household and business you serve, changing your clients' perspective if the value you provide. Instead of seeing you as a transactional professional, they will see you as their trusted advisor—their Discussion Partner.[38]

2. Be the best in your field.

In speaking to groups, I have been using a shopping analogy for years. I like to shop, and there is nothing better than high-end, quality fabric in suits and other clothing. I go to Nordstrom and buy the same items I could have bought at Macy's for 30 percent less because I like the Nordstrom *experience* more. When I walk into Nordstrom, everyone is trained to greet customers. The store is always beautifully decorated, the clothes are displayed in a comfortable environment, and the staff members create a relaxing ambiance.

When I'm on the sales floor, the associates tell me about the new arrivals and the hot sellers. At checkout, the cashier explains why she is taking the time to wrap my clothing in tissue paper and why she folds it a certain way. It's more than just buying a tie or a shirt. It's an *experience* where I feel like I'm the only customer in the store. This is why Nordstrom earns the right to charge 30 percent more than their direct competition—they are the best at what they do.

Be the best at what you do. How can you ramp up ordinary service that customers have come to expect and now create an unrivaled experience? Brainstorm ideas with your team.

3. Use your story to convey to your clients why they should choose and stay with your agency/firm.

Give your prospects and clients the highlights of the company(ies) you represent. Explain how these key elements will benefit them. Introduce the visitors to your team members, and when it's appropriate, let your team members tell their stories. This will help deepen your relationship and engage people with your business.

4. Avoid using insurance and financial services lingo and jargon.

Our industry is filled with acronyms and terms that only agents understand. Just because we know what BI and UIM are does *not* mean our clients do. I've seen too many agents attempt to give the impression of being intelligent by throwing around insurance lingo while speaking with clients. Some clients will just nod and agree with you, and a few will ask questions so you can clarify what you've said, but many of them will walk away more confused than when they arrived.

Don't assume your clients understand your terms. Take the time to explain your products in terms they understand, and then ask the right questions to ensure they do. Help them feel comfortable enough to ask questions without feeling embarrassed. No matter how basic their question might be, say, "Good question. Let me explain . . ." Every conversation anyone on your team has with clients should be conversational, easy to understand, and genuinely compassionate.

5. *Walk your customers through everything you are doing for them now—and are going to do for them after they leave.*

Don't leave any room for interpretation, that is, *mis*interpretation. You may have to use different communication styles with different customers because not all adults learn and understand the same way. Before people walk out the door, review the decisions and next steps. It only takes a few minutes to be sure next steps and expectations are clear to both of you.

Don't assume your customers—even high-level professionals in business, medicine, and the arts—understand the intricacies of insurance and financial planning. Treat them with respect, but avoid assuming they already grasp every concept.

6. *Offer concierge follow-up service.*

We often hear the term *concierge service*, but it's high-level *follow-up* that enhances your customers' overall experience. This doesn't require adding additional staff to the payroll. Just develop a new system for the way your current staff performs follow-up. It might be a simple next-day call to reiterate key discoveries and action items from the previous day's appointment and find out if the customer has questions or concerns.

Take a proactive approach to combat any confusion. Your follow-up is proof to your customers that they matter to you and your team.

These strategies enable you to connect with customers (and potential customers) in ways that demonstrate your care and competence. Trust is the foundation of every relationship, and these six strategies help you demonstrate integrity and offer excellence, which will inspire trust in the people you contact.

CHAPTER 5

SERVICE: YOUR FIRST PRIORITY

If we are going to flip the model upside down, we need to focus on the "gateway to all things insurance and financial services." The gateway is the carrier and agency/firm, not new technology. Some will control the gateway on a global and seamless level, and some will want to control their monoline experts.

In the past, the P&C insurance business focused on giving quotes to compete for part of clients' personal and/or business insurance. The goal was to impress them enough so that the phone would soon ring in your office or for you to ask for permission to give them a comparison quote. The idea was that if you wrote their auto, their home, and their business, you would have the opportunity to later write their life insurance or other business-allied lines such as umbrella, workers' compensation, business owner's policies, employment practices liability insurance (EPLI), and property.

Our process was transactional selling followed by cross-marketing to gain product density with clients (in their households or businesses or both). This model helped our clients get to know us and trust us so they would give us an opportunity to meet all their insurance needs. The law of large numbers worked effectively, and a certain percentage of our clients bought multiple products over a period of time.

However, the expected nirvana of having all insurance and financial services under one roof never materialized. The hope was to cross-sell. If we look back and analyze the data, we see that very few customers bought everything we offered. This left the buying public with multiple advisors—definitely more than one and usually two to five. Over the past 15 or 20 years, many astute carriers, firms, and agencies set up systems and processes to help them cross-sell through letter-writing campaigns, phone calls, review programs, etc. However, the critical mass of customers never bought into "everything under one roof," partly because everything was always (and to a certain degree still is) based on price and limited selection. The fact that clients need to buy a product within a certain price range prohibited them from moving certain lines to another firm, agency, or carrier.

Enter the world of "service first." Servicing and giving advice have become the primary door openers. Once we're in the door, we can offer everything the agency/firm provides. We are "the gateway to all things insurance and financial services": the gateway for service, the gateway for advice, and the gateway for product options. Just because you don't write someone's auto coverage doesn't mean they should go away and never talk to you again. Just because you don't write their home coverage because you're too high or you don't have the right product doesn't mean that prospects should be discarded and that you shouldn't continue the relationship with them. The same goes for business insurance. The same goes for financial services. The same goes for life.

SERVICE VS. SALES

I can't stress it enough—we must move away from quoting as the only entry point to the client's relationship with our agencies/carriers.

This has been the predominant method for starting a relationship in the property & casualty industry. It grew the industry to have more than $670 billion in P&C direct-written premiums.[39] The top 20 carriers in the United States have enjoyed growth and the ability to cross-sell additional business. However, the old way of doing business will never succeed in reaching the Promised Land of having all business for a customer under one roof. And it never will . . . unless you take these actions:

1. Make service your first priority. Treat even your lowest-paying clients like they're guests at a five-star hotel.

2. Become the gateway for service and information on all insurance products and financial services.

3. Align yourself with expertise partners and specialists on your team.

The entryway to the sales funnel is changing in front of our eyes. There used to be only a few entry points:

1. The independent agent

2. The exclusive agent

3. Direct 1-800 numbers

Now, in the digital age, consumers can get quotes 24/7. In the past ten years, a massive amount of media dollars has been spent to get consumer to take action:

» To pick up the phone for a quote

» To go to the computer for a quote

» To use digital devices for a quote

» To call their local agent for a quote

Why do so many carriers focus on giving quotes for auto and home insurance, especially the Exclusive & Direct Carriers? It's very simple—the numbers don't lie. Analytics are everything in business today. If you give 100 quotes, the law of large numbers says that approximately 20 percent of the consumers will purchase. If you're under 20 percent, you need to carefully analyze your rates, systems, processes, and your product in general. If you're over 20 percent, there's another set of business-focused questions to ask to take advantage of the opportunities.

I don't deny that the system has worked. However, being in the P&C business for more than 30 years, I've seen a lot of change. Thirty years ago, 20 years ago, and even 10 years ago, you could make a very good living owning an insurance practice/business and selling only auto and home insurance. Although the carriers wanted greater product density with umbrella, life insurance, business insurance, etc., our success was mainly due to "stickiness," which resulted in customer retention.

There is an undeniable truth that the more products we provide for a household or business, the longer the consumer stays with the agency/firm and the carrier. However, many of the top carriers are overweighted in personal lines. To maintain their dominance and to grow their bottom line, they have been forced to focus more and more on quotes. I don't necessarily find this to be a negative for a carrier, but it's definitely a negative for independent contractors/distributors if they don't sell multiple lines while executing mono-line transactions.

Many carriers are reconsidering having employees lead local offices. Our work in this area shows that both of these management structures can work and grow in the new world of insurance and financial services. The key to success is "creating a seamless ecosystem." The carrier can offer a "one and done" digital experience, they can offer a "one and done" 1-800 experience, or they can offer a "one and done" experience for the customer without contractors of any kind. But a seamless distribution ecosystem has everything. It allows the consumer, whether employee-led or contractor-led, to be in control of how they want to do business: when and how they want to be serviced, as well as when and how they want to purchase protection and other products.

Remember, consumers are driving this change. They're in control. If you want evidence of this, just observe what's going on. We need to provide quotes to more people because fewer people are spending time in our offices or talking with us on the phone. The transformation in how customers get information and quotes has shifted in the blink of an eye—in only the past several years. Experts tell us that the one who gets to the consumer first has the best chance to win, and the sale can be made more easily if you're in the top three for consideration, so think about this: it takes as much as an hour for a customer to get a single quote, and if the customer wants comparisons, he may spend three hours to get three quotes. If comparing quotes will save $50 or even $100, the customer inherently asks if it's worth the hassle of spending three hours to get new quotes every year to save only a few dollars.

People value their time, and they're starting to wake up to the fact that it's better to have someone looking out for their best interests, even if they pay a little more. This is why we believe so strongly that the role of a Discussion Partner/trusted advisor is so valuable to the consumer. Transparency in pricing will win more long-term customers. In addition, putting service first and being open about what customers are getting makes it easier for them to look at service versus cost.

You're no longer in a sales job. Don't put pressure on yourself to *sell* your services. Simply convey to your clients that you care about them and want to represent them. Unfortunately, we've held too closely to this model of sales. But the good news is, there's a wealth of potential for agencies and leaders who update their practices and strategies!

THE IMPORTANCE OF KEY PERFORMANCE INDICATORS

When I talk about the changes in our industry and describe the new world of service as our first priority, people inevitably ask, "Troy, where do I fit in?"

It's a timely question. My answer is, "Think bigger. See more broadly. You're part of a bigger ecosystem, and you want to position yourself as the gateway to all things insurance and financial services. If you're a local distributor, and you're independently owned (or a firm or agency), you need to align yourself with a carrier or carriers as the foundation of your ecosystem. Position yourself as the gateway, a valued Discussion Partner. Put service first so you can compete and thrive in the new world of insurance and financial services."

I don't get tired of telling people the hard news that the old model no longer works—that we've reached the inflection point. We used to make 100 quotes and get 20 new customers, and we never thought about the 80 again. Of the 20, very few bought comprehensive insurance and used our financial planning services. It was always an uphill climb. Now the terrain is even steeper. But this fact isn't a roadblock; it's a launching pad!

If we see ourselves correctly, we can become the gateway for service, the gateway for information, and the gateway for product consideration. To give great service, we need to have an effective platform and a standard of excellence, so set key performance indicators (KPIs) in customer service throughout your organization at an agent level, at a firm level, and at a carrier level.

Carriers and companies in the insurance and financial services worlds have used KPIs for their claims units, marketing, distribution, customer self-service, technology, etc. In all these areas, they understood that to retain business and grow their enterprise, they must constantly use analytics to improve. All good businesses have a set of KPIs to benchmark excellence and progress. In fact, you need to benchmark everything. Most agencies, and most firms that we have had the opportunity to study, don't have rigor around their key performance indicators. To retool and take advantage of the new opportunities today, everyone globally at the local level must set and monitor KPIs and benchmarks.

First, let's benchmark ourselves. Let me list some questions to help you consider direction and progress for you and your team. What are your:

1. KPIs for yourself?

2. Leadership skills?

3. Communication skills?

4. Planning and execution skills?

5. Time-management strategies?

6. Methods for recruiting top talent?

7. Abilities to create and communicate a compelling vision?

8. Financial management (P&L) capabilities?

9. Succession-planning strategies?

Next, take some time to benchmark your business. What are your KPIs for:

1. Incoming calls?

2. Outbound calls?

3. Compliance?

4. Customer self-service?

5. Expertise partnerships?

6. Customer development?

7. Customer retention?

8. Follow-up?

Of course, some key performance indicators are non-negotiable. Today, customers' expectations are higher than ever, and we can't afford to give them less than they expect. In fact, after we assess our capabilities, we need to set a new benchmark to constantly *exceed* their expectations. Our commitment to excellence will help us grow, and it will ensure sustainable growth and longevity.

Don't underestimate the power of preparation. KPIs may seem laborious, but they matter. In fact, they matter a lot. Execution is everything. First, design what you're offering to the marketplace, and then create a road map to execute your plans. From that point, constantly review the analytics, but be careful to analyze the data. A quick survey in an email can give you some valuable information, but don't forget that a lot of people don't fill out those surveys—and those who do aren't always completely honest. I embrace the surveys, but I always need to get down into the trenches to talk to real people.

In other words, my advice is to use the analytics, but test them. Your customers will tell you if you're exceeding their expectations, and they'll tell you if you've positioned things correctly by offering service first. They will also tell you when they aren't happy because you haven't met their expectations. Their loudest and clearest message will come when they find someone else who is a gateway to give them the service they expect.

Research by Esteban Kolsky shows that 13 percent of unhappy customers will share their complaint with 15 or more people. Only one in 25 unhappy customers will complain directly to you.[40] This means you have to actively seek out customers to ask them what you're doing well and what you could do better.

To catch issues preemptively, always ask your clients to come directly to you with any feedback or suggestions. Be on offense, not defense.

Don't ever give your customers an opportunity to look somewhere else! Once they have agreed that you're the gateway to all things for service, advice, and product consideration, be all they expect you to be . . . and more. Trust is the glue of every relationship. Make sure you give people every reason to trust you.

COMMUNICATE CLEAR EXPECTATIONS

Your business should have a continuity procedure book for every department and process in your operation. There should be a job description for every person in every department, including expertise partners, so that everyone is singing from the same song sheet. Develop relationships with outside expertise partners because it makes sense for your business to have someone representing the firm/agency/carrier as a profit center on your payroll.

I suggest two overlapping methods to develop workable job descriptions:

1. First, ask the people in your office to write their own job description. Give them a template that asks them to list responsibilities, reporting procedures, and goals.

2. After they've completed their versions, give them a job description for their specific roles from your carrier or one of the websites that has job descriptions for the insurance industry. Ask them to write their job descriptions again and

make any changes based on the new information provided by the professional version. Then, go over it with them, cast the vision for exemplary service, make any changes in the job description, affirm the employee's contribution, and set a time for a review (in three months, six months, or a year).

EVOLVE FROM TEAM SELLING TO TEAM SERVICING

One definition of *team selling* is "a group of people representing the sales department and other areas in a firm, all sharing a common goal of increased sales." This means every member of your team has a vital role in the success of the business. Here are some of the advantages of team selling:[41]

1. The team approach has many sets of eyes on the process, so strengths can be maximized and flaws can be identified and corrected more quickly.

2. Customers have contact with more than one person, making the local company seem larger and more global than it is.

3. Team members who may have been used only for administrative tasks may demonstrate hidden talents and excellence in service and sales.

4. Customers will have more than one person to contact when they have a need.

5. More people involved in selling and service lowers the overall cost of sales calls.

Because of the complexity and abundance of products and services available today, it's impossible for one person to be an expert in all of them. When you offer many different agents' expertise in various products to your customers, they benefit from a more robust array of knowledge and insight.

Your team is your greatest resource, and team selling is essential. The independent agency system has used this concept for years, especially for larger accounts. There are myriad examples of team selling being used effectively in the worlds of life insurance and financial services. Employee benefits carriers and firms use team selling to onboard their customers. Many of the exclusive/multiline companies have mirrored this process to write mid-sized and larger accounts.

Team selling is popular because it's effective. Associations like the GAMA Foundation have spent much time researching and helping firms execute this capability at all levels. The fact is, it doesn't matter how large or small your company is; everyone needs to use this concept. But we need to flip the concept upside down and call it "team servicing." Lead with service first to ensure maximum sales and profitability for everyone involved with the customer.

To what extent is your service unparalleled in your niche or in your geographical area? If you can build this reputation, you won't have to go looking for clients. Why would a client choose your agency, firm, carrier, or distribution alliance over another one? Service—nothing less than unrivaled service provided by team members whose expertise, knowledge, and experience covers all bases. Service first! Service always!

CHAPTER 6

MASTER OF ALL

Most of us in the insurance and financial services industry feel like a "jack of all trades, master of none." That is, we feel pressure to know everything and be able to do anything for our clients. This expectation may have been reasonable in the past, but those simpler times are gone.

One reason is that the number and complexity of insurance and financial services products has increased. Another reason is that our customers now have more complex needs. They own more, they earn more, and they desire more. As the complexity of their needs change, so does the complexity of the products and services we offer.

Today, you need to be licensed to sell many intricate instruments. If you plan to be successful among the onslaught of rapid change, you'd better have some highly effective strategies to increase your knowledge base and become a master of every aspect of the business.

So how do you master it all? You can't do it alone. With today's vast offerings in insurance and financial services, it's simply not possible for one agent or advisor to be an expert in everything. We can't be the master *of* all, but we can become the master *over* all. How do you keep your arms wrapped around all the things that are important to your clients and to the health of your carrier/firm? How do you keep informed of all the changes and updates in the industry? How do you ensure nothing falls through the cracks?

The answer: The only way to master it all in today's environment is to collaborate with more people and use better systems. In my book, *Discussion Partner,* I used this illustration:

> If my clients, Mr. and Mrs. Templeton, buy a Cessna airplane, I am going to be thrilled for them, but I'm not an expert in aviation insurance. And if they buy a horse farm, I will be excited for them, but I'm not an expert in equine insurance, either. I won't be able to personally write coverage for their new asset, yet I know people who *are* experts in those areas. This is why collaboration is so important for reps and advisors today.
>
> When the Templetons buy that new plane, here's what I will tell them:
>
> I'm so excited for you! I know you've both been wanting that plane for a long time. I have expertise in aviation insurance right at my fingertips. I just talked with Joe Jones, who has written a lot of policies for personal and business aircraft. Let's set up an appointment so we all can meet at a time that's convenient for you. This is the type of service I give to all our clients. I just want you to know that I appreciate your calling me for everything that comes up in both your personal life and business life. We are here to help you any way we can.[42]

I don't have the aviation expert on my payroll, but I have access to such experts through partnerships and relationships, whether they compensate me or not. I'm not handing the client over to the expertise partner; I'm serving as the gateway to connect my client with that expert. I may be handing the ball off to someone else, but I'm still the quarterback.

When you surround yourself with people who have extraordinary expertise in all types of professional services, you can tell your clients, "I've partnered with Joe Jones, who is an expert in this field, and we're going to use his expertise on this coverage."[43]

EYES ON THE PRIZE

Many companies today, whether exclusive or independent, are distracted by rapid advances in technology and changes in the industry. Instead, they should be keeping their eyes on the prize of *continuous growth*. The hundreds of millions of dollars currently being spent on innovation without regard for a strategic endgame will only lead to incremental and temporary success.

I grew up in a world that was both exclusive and independent. I understand why exclusive agents hoarded personal information about their customers—they didn't want the carrier who "owned" the customers to have any way to contact them directly through mail, email, or phone. Conversely, independent agents truly did "own" their customers, so they had good reasons to withhold this information.

Today, the slate has been wiped clean, and anyone can instantly get all the information we used to hoard. If I want to know something about somebody, I can get it: phone numbers, addresses, occupations, and history. Now you can know a person's driving habits, where they park their car, their income, and other information that used to be off-limits.

The prize is our ability to create stronger relationships with our customers. We now have access to more information, and we can get it more quickly. What we do with it is up to us. If we choose to pay close attention to those details, they will form the foundation of trusted, lasting relationships.

FILL THE GAPS

I was never licensed to sell financial services. However, I knew we needed to have someone offer this important service to our clients. To fill this gap, I had my top producers licensed, and they offered the services and kept the commissions. Our clients either didn't know or didn't care that I wasn't the one who held the license, and the ones who knew didn't care because their needs were being satisfied . . . all under one roof.

It didn't matter to me that I wasn't receiving monetary compensation. What mattered is that client retention increased, and we deepened our relationships with our clients. It also mattered that my top producers felt trusted and made more money—a combination that produces loyalty and enthusiasm.

All roads should lead to helping people and businesses with protection and growth. Combining protection and growth strategies makes the most sense to your customers. It allows them to receive a comprehensive and strategic plan for their future from one trusted source. In that scenario, there's less margin for error. Together, you can create a holistic view of their needs and goals and design a portfolio tailored for their family and business needs.

UP YOUR GAME

Today, customers expect us to show up with every conceivable option in our bags. This means you have to "up your game." It's imperative that you have access to *all* the information, systems, processes, products, and services to help your clients grow, both in their personal lives and in their businesses.

And today, their needs go far beyond the basics. You should know everything you can about your customers, from where they work to what they do for leisure to where their passions lie. Catalog all this information in the electronic files you keep, and use it to connect with them on deeper levels to strengthen your relationships.

For instance, if one of your clients is heavily involved in a nonprofit organization, find out how you can get involved. Offer to donate cases of water to their child's next sporting event. Hang flyers or display cards to promote their events or small businesses. But be genuine. Involve yourself only in organizations you believe in and whose values align with yours.

Giving starts a cycle of trust and generosity. Show that you're interested in more than financial gain. You need to believe in your clients' heartfelt goals, not just in the premiums they pay to your firm.

OWN YOUR DAY

How many times have you laid your head down at night, only to have your brain go into overdrive? Panic creeps in when you realize you forgot to do something important—or ten things that are important!

I used to keep myself up for hours at night, going over my to-do list again and again so I wouldn't forget it the next day. Inevitably, the next day would start out on hyperspeed, and I would completely forget about my list, only to let it drive me insane again that night.

Owning your day goes beyond writing a to-do list or even adding tasks to your calendar. It involves dedication and planning. It means defining your week, month, and year in advance and constantly checking up on progress toward your goals. And before you say, "I don't have time to plan," think back to all those sleepless nights. It's impossible to master something that doesn't exist. If you don't know what the plan is for your business and for yourself, how can you ever master it?

When clients hesitate to take the steps we've recommended and say, "I don't have time to plan," we always encourage them to take time because it's so important. I encourage you to look in the mirror; that may be your excuse, too. Actually, we don't have time *not* to plan!

What do you need to block time for today? What are your non-negotiables? How are you using your time more wisely than you were a year ago?

You need to retool your business. First you need to retool yourself, and then retool your team. To own your day, you need to become an expert in research and communication. You don't need to be an expert in every field of insurance and financial services, but you need to develop the ability to find those people and acquire the right information for your customers.

Here's the bottom line: if you're going to continue to run a transactional selling firm, you need to be the best you can be to close as much business as possible. If, on the other hand, you're going to be a trusted advisor/Discussion Partner, you must know everything about your customers. Once you know them well, you can offer them the information they need that's available in the marketplace. You can offer your products that are commissioned, but clients will make the decision that's best for their families and businesses.

USE CONSISTENT PROCESSES

Processes and procedures are constantly changing. New software programs will be integrated, marketing campaigns will come and go, and corporate infrastructures will be overhauled. These changes are all out of your control, but they will directly affect your business.

So how do you ensure minimal disruption to your business when a new process or procedure is forced on you? The key is to maintain the fundamentals of operating your business. This means having systems and procedures in place for all the situations and events that occur daily in your office, as well as for the surprises that pop up.

How can you create effective and flexible systems? By investing time with your team to make everything *uniform* in your processes. Consistency is king.

Gladly's Customer Expectations 2019 report found that consistency is key to a good customer experience, with 62 percent of consumers saying it's very important to not have to repeat previous interactions. In fact, respondents to the survey valued consistency higher than being able to use their preferred channel.[44]

The reason chain restaurants have become so popular is that you can get your favorite meal in a different city, state, or country and know it's going to be exactly the same each time. Your business should be no different. Your customers should have the same experience whether they speak with you directly or with anyone else on your team.

Incorporate standards in your business, such as setting up everyone's desk the same way and ensuring that your entire team uses the same verbiage when they speak with clients—which you can accomplish by writing scripts for every possible conversation your team will have with clients. This will help ensure that everyone on your team conducts client meetings with the same level of professional excellence, which in turn ensures that your agency's value proposition and priorities are being communicated in a consistent way each time by each team member. Put procedures into place for handling incoming and outgoing calls, client complaints, scheduling appointments, and so on.

Master the way your customers perceive your office. Your goal is to make every interaction pleasant and productive and to eliminate all confusion and frustration by offering your customers the same positive experience every time they work with your office.

SURROUND YOURSELF WITH GREATNESS

We know that a chain is only as strong as its weakest link. In ancient times, rulers of kingdoms didn't know everything. To lead and provide for their people, they needed access to wise men, expert tradesmen, commodities, builders, and generals. It's the same way today—none of us knows everything.

At this moment, you may be the weakest link in your agency and not even realize it—not because you don't produce at a high level or meet with your clients effectively, but because you are failing to surround yourself with all the proper relationships you need to propel your business into the future.

Start first with the people in your building. Do you have the right team members on board? If the answer is no, it's time to replace them. Once you have your internal team dialed in, work on your external connections. Create relationships and synergies with other firms in your industry—firms you can go to when your customer has needs outside your expertise and offerings.

Don't stop there. Join trade clubs, chambers of commerce, church groups, or other professional groups to cultivate relationships throughout your community and across other industry lines.

Our industry will always require that we know at least a little about everything. While basic insurance and financial services are simple, our customers have multifaceted, complex needs. We will never be able to master every product and service required to run our businesses and serve our customers. However, we can master our oversight of it all and ensure that it runs in a smooth and productive manner.

We are the rulers, and this is our kingdom. Put in the work today to create a business that will not only grow but thrive in the future.

CHAPTER 7

WHERE TO FIND THE RIGHT CUSTOMERS: AN ORGANIC APPROACH

We see the word *organic* on just about everything we purchase today. *Organic* used to refer primarily to foods grown without chemicals or livestock raised with no antibiotics, but now we see the term on labels on everything from personal hygiene products to cleaning supplies and even building materials.

A recent TechSci Research study found that sales of organic foods are rapidly increasing and are projected at an annual growth rate of more than 14 percent over the next few years.[45] The research didn't measure customers' preferences for all of the other organic products available in the market, but we can assume it's significant. Undoubtedly, our preference for natural or organic products has grown in recent years and will continue to grow.

What makes organic such a popular alternative? When we think of organic, we think pure. You're getting something natural that hasn't been subjected to toxins or other chemicals—as close as possible to the way nature intended: pristine, unadulterated, and healthy. Restaurants are part of this movement as they offer "farm to table" ingredients grown locally and with a minimal amount of handling along the way.

You might be asking yourself, *What does this have to do with my insurance and financial services business?* Well, I'm glad you asked. Whether I'm in front of a crowd speaking, leading a webinar, or contributing to a roundtable discussion, the topics of leads and lead generation inevitably come up. Local agency storefronts struggle to find effective methods to secure leads for prospective clients. According to *Insurance Leads Guide,* the average lead costs a business approximately $20 to $50, with no guarantee of securing a sale. In fact, in most cases there's no guarantee that you are the only business in your market to receive the lead. Many companies sell the same leads to multiple businesses without any disclosure.[46]

A recent article from Hubspot regarding sales statistics reported that it takes an average of eighteen calls to reach your buyer. It also cited that only 50 percent of your prospects are a good fit for what you sell.[47] While these numbers are accurate, don't allow them to be discouraging. The primary reason businesses fail to convert a lead into a client is purely in their initial approach. First impressions are the most lasting . . . and the most important. You want your first impression to be the first step in creating a long-term, meaningful relationship—you're showing that you're not merely a transactional salesperson trying to meet a sales quota.

In June 2019, Tyson Quick, Founder and CEO of Instapage, posted a blog on personalized marketing. He said 80 percent [of customers] say they are more likely to do business with a company if it offers personalized experiences. In addition, 90 percent [of customers] claim they find personalization appealing.[48] People want to do business with someone they know and trust. They want a personalized experience, and they expect to be treated as more than just a checkbook and an account number. They want real relationship with professionals.

For years, agencies around the globe have used a system I created, "The Introductions Program," to generate solid leads with high customer conversion. The internal structure of the program has morphed over the years to keep up with market and industry changes; however, the fundamentals and the delivery have remained constant. This is a program that centers around organic growth of your business through a personalized approach.

THE INTRODUCTIONS PROGRAM

Let me describe a simple and effective process to make the most of introductions:

» Set times on your calendar each day to go outside your office on four introduction appointments.

» I recommend going on appointments on your way to work, to and from lunch, and on your way home.

» Keep them short. Your in-person appointment or call should last three minutes or less.

» Schedule a follow-up after your initial in-person meeting.

» Add the prospect to your ongoing marketing schedule to create an ongoing workflow for yourself.

» Make a phone call to each prospective client in two weeks to ask permission to start a file on them.

» Catalogue their personal and business insurance and financial services information. Follow up with them at the
right time.

» Catalogue details such as number of employees, personal
hobbies, and information about family members (names,
ages of kids, anniversary date, etc.).

In some cases, you won't be able to obtain an appointment
with the prospective client. That's okay. Put them back on your
calendar to follow up again. The key is to never take the prospect
off of your calendar, unless, of course, they specifically make this
request. Stay consistent and continually reach out to them over
the year—not to always sell them something, but to check in and
see how they're doing. You'll find that over time your prospect
will appreciate the personalized attention, and many will become
clients.

Use this organic approach with prospective clients. It doesn't
have any toxins; instead, it's fresh, healthy, and productive.

CHAPTER 8

BECOME A LIFELONG LEARNER

In my book, *Discussion Partner: A Radical Transformation to Unrivaled Service in the Insurance Industry*, I point out that to be successful in the future, you need to be willing to adapt quickly. As we've seen, the way companies, including those in insurance and financial services, are doing business is rapidly changing. It's no longer "business as usual." We not only need to navigate the tsunami of change for our own businesses; we also need to lead our clients through the same tsunami.

To move past the inflection point—that moment in time when the existing model no longer works—we need to stay up-to-date on changes within the companies we do business with and those companies that directly affect our industry. The stream of new information is coming fast, and you can't afford to fall behind. If lifelong learning wasn't one of your core values before, it needs to be now.

With just a click of their search buttons, current and potential customers are barraged with an overwhelming amount of information. Becoming an expert in your field will allow you to help them sort through the information overload and gain their confidence as a trusted advisor. Lifelong learning has never been more important than it is today. Shooting from the hip or "winging it" may have been acceptable in the past, but it's no longer an option.

You will be hard-pressed to find any prospect or an existing client who hasn't done some preliminary research on our industry offerings. Your job is to remove the clutter of information and explain your value in a language people will understand. This will alleviate frustrations and enable your clients to make informed decisions for their families' and/or businesses' personalized needs.

How do you work on uncluttering the insurance world for your clients? What does this look like practically for you?

Intentional and purposeful learning should become a permanent component of your business plan. In fact, it can become as habitual as unlocking the front door of your office and turning on the computer. Customers are demanding more astute and informed advisors in all professional industries. Our authority, based on industry knowledge, must convey the higher value of personalized service over the perceived faster and cheaper online options. We must make learning a daily priority to keep us relevant as advisors so we can offer our customers the powerful combination of our knowledge and that of our expertise partners.

Let me be clear: This advice doesn't contradict the need to find and develop relationships with expertise partners. It means that you continue to learn and grow in your professional excellence as you enlist experts in other fields. Both need to happen ... and happen continually.

Today, change is happening so fast that people in every facet of the business world need to make it a priority to keep learning new information and acquiring new skills. In an article in *Harvard Business Review*, Josh Bersin and Marc Zao-Sanders comment on a survey of corporate executives:

> As automation, AI, and new job models reconfigure the business world, lifelong learning has become accepted as an economic imperative. Eighty percent of CEOs now believe the need for new skills is their biggest business challenge. For employees, research now shows that opportunities for development have become the second most important factor in workplace happiness (after the nature of the work itself). At the most fundamental level, we are a neotenic species, born with an instinct to learn throughout our lives. So it makes sense that at work we are constantly looking for ways to do things better; indeed, the growth-mindset movement is based on this human need. And whereas recruitment is an expensive, zero-sum game (if company A gets the star, company B does not), learning is a rising tide that lifts all boats.[49]

MAKE IT HAPPEN

Here are five simple ways to integrate lifelong learning into any busy schedule:

1. Make an appointment with yourself.

Pick a time during the day to block out one hour in your schedule to devote to study. This can be any time of the day—before, during, or after work. Keep the mindset that this appointment is set in stone. Don't allow yourself or your staff to schedule anything on top of it, reschedule it, or remove it. This appointment is just as important as meeting with a client—and maybe more important.

2. Take advantage of company- and industry-sponsored webinars and video calls.

There's no shortage of these opportunities in our industry. This is a great way to get excellent information on relevant subjects, as well as input from peers. One caveat: not all information is useful. If you find that the subject matter doesn't apply or appeal to you, simply disconnect and find content that's relevant to you.

3. Multitask.

I like to download Audibles or YouTube videos and listen to them while I exercise. Take a few minutes to load your device with powerful and informative videos, audio files, or digital books. Next time you find yourself eating at your desk, waiting in line at the bank, working out, or sitting in traffic, turn on one of the selections from your library. These quick injections of learning add up over the days, weeks, and months.

4. Go outside your comfort zone.

Although it's very important to stay informed within your industry, it is equally important to expand your boundaries. Explore ideas from other fields, and discover how you can adapt them to your own business. In addition to a wide range of business resources, read or listen to philosophy, satire, biographies, history, or anthropology. The "human struggle" hasn't changed over the past two thousand years. You will find that no matter how old or new the content is, some part of it will resonate with you.

5. Embrace digital minimalism.

Be open to disconnecting from your devices for some period of time each day. Part of lifelong learning is examining ourselves more deeply. Put it on your schedule to shut out the noise for a set time each day so you can reflect and rebalance yourself. Ask yourself some good questions, such as: "What could I have said or done differently during today's sales meeting?" "How can I improve my communication or leadership skills?" "How can I apply current industry changes to my business?" Find solace in the quiet and stillness of time with yourself.

START SMALL, BUT START

Don't allow yourself to become overwhelmed. There is no need to order the past twelve issues of every insurance and financial services periodical or go into debt filling up your Amazon cart.

Today is Day One. Start small and ease into it. Pick one or two subjects that interest you, and learn more about them. Focus on these until you have a good handle on the topics. There's a reason the term the "building blocks of learning" exists. Think of learning as a giant brick wall that has only begun to be constructed. One brick does not a wall make, but over time, the bricks start to add up, and the wall becomes tall and impenetrable.

A small change in your schedule, along with purposeful dedication, will have a huge impact on your confidence, your business, and your relationships with your clients.

DON'T WAIT

Years ago, Everett Rogers wrote a landmark book called *Diffusion of Innovations*. In it, he identified five categories of responses to change: innovators, early adopters, early majority, late majority, and laggards. I appreciate those who are bold, creative innovators. Most of us don't fall into that category, but here's the truth: If you aren't an early adopter to take advantage of the changes in insurance and financial services, you'll be left behind. I know this makes some of you uncomfortable, but it's my job to give you a nudge—and maybe a push—to get you going.

Don't wait on the sidelines. Get in the game.

Don't be stubborn. Adapt or die.

CHAPTER 9

WHEN THE GAME CHANGES, CHANGE THE WAY YOU PLAY THE GAME

As consumers, we're constantly yearning for a better experience from the companies we do business with. We want more variety, faster delivery, and an overall smooth buying experience. This is an obvious and incontrovertible truth.

Why, then, do so many professionals fail to deliver this level of service to their customers and clients . . . especially those in the insurance and financial services arena? Let me ask two important questions: Why have so many in this industry become complacent and content with the status quo? And what are the paralyzing factors that have kept our industry so far behind the times?

The answer to both questions is that our industry has positioned itself in a particular—and severely limiting—way. In the past (and maybe even still today), most of us sold insurance and financial services *as transactions*. The astute practitioners among us were able to give great advice on a few specific products and sell these products in the belief that our customers were adequately covered. In most cases, they were; however, we didn't provide the full range of information our customers needed because our offerings were limited to what was in our toolbox.

We need a bigger toolbox, and we need to partner with providers who have tools that aren't in our box. Let me reiterate some points we covered in earlier chapters and apply them to the relationships with people we encounter every day.

WEAN YOURSELF FROM QUOTES AND MERE TRANSACTIONS

Today we must look at the bigger picture. We need to look at the full view of our clients' needs, a 360-degree view. In the age of the Internet, providing limited information just won't cut it. We need to leave no stone unturned to provide all the options for a complete portfolio of coverages and services that best fits a customer's family and/or business needs. In addition, we must be open to the fact that sometimes this coverage or these services are outside the wheelhouse of our offerings.

Believing in your product is imperative, but believing that one size fits all—and that everyone needs only our product—is delusional.

It's time to take a hard look at how we currently do business. This is, and will always be, a sales-driven industry—that is, we will always need the transaction of the sale. But does this mean that every interaction with a client must lead to a sale? No, of course not.

Let's look at other businesses for a different point of view. The dentist brings in a patient to clean her teeth. Does every patient need a whitening kit, a tooth pulled, or a root canal? Of course not. The dentist cleans her teeth and does a thorough examination before suggesting any other procedures. Patients need different services at different times. Let's expand even further on this example. Maybe the patient has crooked teeth—and she likes them that way! She doesn't see any need to straighten her teeth. Would the dentist keep pushing her to use a service she doesn't want? No, he wouldn't. The dentist is a professional and prescribes only the required services to keep the patient healthy.

In the same way, listen to your customers. Put their needs above your desire to sell. Don't worry about production; you'll quickly discover that the numbers will work themselves out because a certain percentage of the people will buy from you, and all of them will feel understood and served, so they'll recommend you to their friends. The key is to approach the right customer in the right way from the start. Your target customer is one who looks at all the options and is willing to pay more for the value of a trusted advisor.

It's critical to the growth of your business that you begin weaning yourself from the temptation of phone quoting and transactional selling. Instead, focus your initial interaction—and all successive interactions—on building relationships. A foundation of trust between you and your customers is the key to your business success. You want to be the one (and the only one) they think of for all their insurance and financial services needs.

So where do you find these customers, and how do you attract them? Actually, you're already having interactions with them every day. They are the parents you say "Hi" to when dropping off your kids at school. They are in your leads group. They go to your church. They are the bank teller, your plumber, your mechanic, and the owner of your favorite sandwich shop. We interact with potential customers and potential employees many times every day. Unfortunately, we get stuck in our routine and often run on autopilot as we make our way through the world around us.

When we stop and make a conscious effort to see the people whose lives ours intersect each day, we realize the real potential of these casual connections.

THREE SUGGESTIONS

To make the most of your opportunities to connect with people, let me offer three concrete suggestions:

1. Use your daily routine to your advantage.

You would never walk into your dry cleaners to pick up your shirts for the week and say, "Hey, look, I put together a quote for you to buy insurance from me." But many of the times you go there, you have a few minutes to ask about the business owner's kids, how business is going, what they did last weekend, and genuinely care about him.

Sooner or later, these friendly interactions earn you the right to ask for an appointment in your place of business to get to know them on a deeper level—but again, not to try selling them something immediately.

It's crucial to set the tone for a relationship-based approach to clients so they see you as a trusted advisor rather than merely a transactional salesperson.

Think of the example of your interactions with the people who work at the dry cleaners and apply it to all your relationships throughout your community. Who are the first ten people who come to mind with whom you could deepen your relationship and earn the right for an appointment? Start there, and keep expanding your circle of meaningful connections.

2. Use The 360-degree approach for the initial presentation.

Let's assume you've applied the first suggestion: you've earned the right for an initial appointment. You didn't earn it by being a pushy, fast-talking salesperson, so don't blow it by immediately trying to sell something to your new prospect/customer.

The initial meeting should be a presentation of you, your business, and the company(ies) you represent. It's also an opportunity to get to know your customer better. Besides collecting all the necessary information, such as how many cars and homes they own, as well as life insurance policies and financial services they currently have, you want to go deeper to understand their heartfelt goals. What are their passions? Are they involved in community outreach, global charities, or other causes? Do they sit on any boards or coach any teams? What keeps them up at night, and what gives them the most satisfaction? Only when you discover their concerns and priorities can you find out what they need from you. All this information is necessary if you want to ensure you are providing a holistic approach to your customers' needs.

3. Examine your product and services offerings.

As you meet with prospective customers, you'll uncover needs for a product or service outside the offerings of your current company(ies). This isn't a roadblock; it's an opportunity to align yourself with other professionals within and outside of our industry to ensure that your customers' specific needs are met.

We need to face the fact that we can't *be* all things to all people, but we can still *provide solutions* for all things to all people.

Here's the bottom line: we need to strive to offer advice on products we sell directly, understand and advise on products for which we receive no commission, have expertise partners who can provide advice and products we don't offer, and let people make the decision that's best for their family and/or their business.

In addition, we can provide value-added services to make each customer's life easier. If we pay attention, we'll see that grocery stores and big-box stores do this on a local level. For instance, they offer additional products and services, such as a pharmacy, a bank, or a coffee shop in their stores to keep more of their customers' business under one roof. To compete in the Amazon.com world of today, we need to also offer products and services that are outside our wheelhouse. Offering oversight and guidance will ensure that we keep all our customers' needs under one roof . . . *our* roof.

In a provocative article in *Inc.,* Mareo McCracken reviews research on customer satisfaction and comes to some startling conclusions—startling for him, but perhaps not for us. He explains that many companies desperately try to exceed customer expectations, but they take the wrong path. The study found . . .

> . . . that when trying to please a customer companies often focus on exceeding customer expectations by giving away free services, extending payment terms, offering free products, or refunding a customer—and the results are not what you would expect. The customers reported that their loyalty is only slightly higher than if the vendor

would just meet or satisfy their needs, rather than trying to exceed them. The extra effort is usually wasted.

Customer loyalty, the study discovered, significantly rises when the focus is on "making it easy" for them to do business with us. He gets very practical:

Easy should mean different things in different industries. Yet, if you can answer these questions positively, you know you're on the right track.

» Is it *easy* to buy from you?

» Is it *easy* to solve problems with your team?

» Is it *easy* to share information?

» Is it *easy* to manage projects together?[50]

That's the goal of our interactions with customers. The Internet has already made it easy for them to find and purchase insurance products, so our job is to make their connections with us even easier as we answer these questions.

PROVIDE SERVICE BEYOND EXPECTATIONS

The most effective marketing in the modern world doesn't merely describe products or services; it shows how these offerings add *value* to a person's life.

We can follow this example by looking to help our customers in ways that are beyond what they normally expect from us. The opportunities are almost endless. We can provide information about a wide range of topics that interest them. This shows that we care about *them*, not just their policies and premiums.

For instance, if you really want to help your clients today, help them *declutter*. They get so much mail on every policy and product they purchase. The carrier or company sends mail that's important, but beyond the information that's necessary and compliant, they send mountains of extraneous information that don't need to be retained. Our customers generally keep all the information in a file or a stack, and it's daunting for them to decide what's important and what's not. When they look for a piece of paper they need, they get frustrated when it's hidden in piles of useless mail. A year's stack of papers creates a no-win situation for the consumer.

How did we get so much paperwork? Well, there's always the compliance issue, and that's non-negotiable. However, much of the paperwork sent in the mail includes junk mail, advertising, and back-of-the-envelope information. I remember when a company always printed real estate advertising on the backs of envelopes. They saw it as an inexpensive way to inform people about houses for sale in their area. Most people looked at the ad and threw the envelope away, but a few were interested and kept it. However, the envelope was an odd size and was awkward to keep up with. It seemed like a great idea, but it proved to be a cumbersome marketing solution.

You can add value by creating a process that declutters your customers' desks and files. Make them a clean hard file for each product, and offer to give them an e-file for their desktop or device. Let your customer know you will keep copies and file them in their confidential file, with their permission, of course. That way, when they have a question regarding any insurance or financial services product, you will be able to answer it based on their most current copy.

This system will also help you catalog what they *don't* have—that is, the gaps in their coverage. This information helps you have a deeper and more meaningful conversation each time you meet.

This is a simple service, but it's a tangible way to make people's lives easier. It's a value-added service. Let's help our clients declutter their insurance and financial services information. Let's help them create a file as a go-forward way of doing business for their families and/or their businesses. Let's help make their lives easier and create a reason for them to see us each year.

DON'T BLINK!

One thing I know for certain is that the world around us is changing at a rapid pace, and it's not going to slow down. Don't snooze, and don't blink, or you'll certainly miss something!

Now is the time to recognize the inflection point and get on the front end of change. Don't be one of the people who sits back and waits for things to go back to the way they were. Those days have come and gone. If you don't make the necessary changes now, you risk your business being cannibalized by a forward-thinking competitor.

A world of opportunities is open to you. The rapidly changing insurance and financial services industry presents both a challenge and an opportunity. Those who are timid never seize the opportunities, but those who anticipate changes and take action will ride the wave of change to greater success.

CHAPTER 10

THE FUTURE'S SO BRIGHT, YOU GOTTA WEAR SHADES

Do you remember that catchy song from the '80s from Timbuk 3? The lyrics go, "Things are going great, and they're only getting better. The future's so bright, I gotta wear shades."[51]

It was a goofy song, but it had a positive message—actually, an accurate one. I believe this is one of the very best times to be in the insurance and financial services industry. Opportunities are overflowing, and we are positioned like never before to offer our customers coverage and services across multiple channels, called an *omnichannel*. The prefix *omni* is derived from the Latin word *omnis*, meaning "all."

MediaBeacon defines and describes the concept:

The term *omnichannel* is defined as the integration of the different channels available to consumers for research-ing, purchasing, and communicating with brands. It is a term that has become increasingly more important as consumers become empowered to interact with brands on multiple platforms and at every stage in the customer cycle, from becoming aware of the brand to turning into a brand advocate.[52]

Another word we're hearing a lot is *multichannel,* although this concept isn't as comprehensive and seamless as *omnichannel.* In an article for *The Future of Customer Engagement and Commerce,* Branwell Moffat explains:

> Although both multi and omnichannel involve selling across multiple physical and digital channels, the key difference is how the customer experience is joined up across those channels. A traditional multichannel re-tailer may have a website and physical stores. These two channels are generally very siloed and have very little in-teraction with one another. Today's consumers do not tend to see a brand in silos. They are likely to have multi-ple touchpoints with a retailer and expect their customer journey between each touchpoint or channel should be seamless. I don't see a retailer's stores and website as dif-ferent companies or silos, but often my experience across one channel is completely separated from another chan-nel. I want to be able to interact with the brand online, through social, on my mobile, or in-store, and I want each of these interactions to be unified."[53]

Our task—and our opportunity—is to become *omnichannel* providers so our customers see us as the go-to resources for all their insurance and financial services needs. Don't wait for your carrier(s) to create the experience for you. Leverage any and every opportunity you can to make this a reality in your business model.

As noted in the section about retooling in chapter 2, many of the mergers and acquisitions we have seen recently in the industry are focused on promoting product-mix modernization. We have the ability to service and provide advice on all our customers' needs, protecting what they have today while securing their financial future. Our capacity to grow our businesses has never been better. The industry is poised for ongoing mergers and partnerships that will continue to increase the reach of carriers and the local agency or firm.

The wave of the future is consolidation, but today many customers have separate advisors for their insurance needs and their financial needs (and sometimes multiple advisors for each). This made sense in the past, when insurance companies either didn't offer financial services or had limited offerings. But today, we have access to either the same offerings—or comparable ones—as the big trading firms. It no longer makes sense for our clients to have two or more separate advisors. Think about it: we don't have two family attorneys, two CPAs, or two primary physicians—we have one of each. We rely on one professional to handle our needs in a specific area of life or business. Why should it be any different in our industry?

There are several significant benefits to customers who have a single advisor. In "Simplify Your Investing Life with Fewer Accounts," Barbara Friedberg lists these: "Your portfolio is easier to track and manage, costs can be kept to a minimum, no one needs multiple 401(k) accounts, withdrawals are simpler, and your caregivers and heirs will thank you." Friedberg concludes, "Although the exact number of accounts an investor should have depends on the individual, one principle remains the same for everyone: winnowing that number to the bare minimum gives you greater control and simplicity, advantages that especially matter once you retire."[54]

When our customers buy insurance protection, they often tell us that they're loyal to their health insurance and benefits provider at work, loyal to their property & casualty provider, and loyal to their life insurance provider. Instead, it would make sense for customers to have one place to go for advice if they could get it all under one roof. It would be convenient and helpful for them to know that someone is overseeing all the available resources to help them find their best options in the entire insurance marketplace—options not offered as commission products for the firms representing them, and options for alternative methods to mitigate risk.

Why do some of our customers still have more than one advisor? One of the most common reasons we hear from customers is, "I like to have two advisors to ensure I'm diversified." But as you know, diversification doesn't come from having more than one advisor. More often than not, we find that a customer invests in the same options, just with two different advisors—which means they're paying two different commissions.

As a "one-stop-shop," our customers know us, and we know them. We understand their hopes and dreams, as well as their fears. Our strong connections enable us to retain their business and offer additional products. In the future, auto insurance may radically change due to ride-sharing, telematics, and self-driving cars. If this portion of our business declines, we'll need to make up for it by offering other quality products and providing the finest service our customers can imagine. We can do it. We *have* to do it.

We have an advantage over the big trading firms: we can offer our clients more than just stock options and trade tips. We offer protection for what they have today, and we can develop relationships to know them, their families, their businesses, and their unique needs to help them achieve what they want for tomorrow. We have the ability to get a 360-degree view of their households and businesses, and we offer protection and services to assist at every angle.

See how bright the future is for us? Now is the time to leverage our advantage in the marketplace. Each of us can become a highly trusted, well-connected and customer-service-focused advisor to whom our clients will come for all their needs.

Transaction-based selling is a dinosaur. Now that we have reached the inflection point—that moment in time when the old model no longer works—we have unlimited potential for providing unrivaled service and serving a valuable role in serving our clients and protecting everything that's valuable and precious to them.

Don't miss the opportunity!

ENDNOTES

1. "Walmart Does Not Boost Employment or Retail Sales," University of Illinois at Chicago, January 8, 2010, https://www.newswise.com/articles/study-walmart-does-not-boost-employment-or-retail-sales32.

2. A. J. Agrawal, "The 'Amazon Effect': How Ecommerce Will Change in 2019 and Beyond," *Entrepreneur*, https://www.entrepreneur.com/article/325556.

3. "Life Insurance Industry Now at a Crossroads," Accenture, September 21, 2018, https://insuranceblog.accenture.com/life-insurance-industry-now-at-a-crossroads.

4. "What Should Insurers Do Today to Prepare for Tomorrow? America's Insurance Outlook 2019," Ernst & Young, 2019, https://assets.ey.com/content/dam/ey-sites/ey-com/en_gl/topics/insurance/insurance-pdfs/ey-insurance-outlook-americas.pdf.

5. "Agents of the Future: The Evolution of Property and Casualty Insurance Distribution," McKinsey & Company, 2013, https://www.mckinsey.com/~/media/mckinsey/dotcom/client_service/financial%20services/latest%20thinking/insurance/agents_of_the_future_the_evolution_of_property_and_casualty_insurance_distribution.ashx.

6. "Digital Insurance in 2018: Driving Real Impact with Digital and Analytics," McKinsey & Company, 2018, https://www.mckinsey.com/~/media/McKinsey/Industries/Financial%20Services/Our%20Insights/Digital%20insurance%20in%202018%20Driving%20real%20impact%20with%20digital%20and%20analytics/Digital-insurance-in-2018.ashx.

7. Neil Spector, "Property/Casualty Insurance Results: 2017," ISO, 2018, http://www.pciaa.net/pciwebsite/common/page/attachment/76044.

8. James T Scanlon, Karen R. Terry, and Maggie Leyes, "2018 Insurance Barometer," LIMRA, April 9, 2018, https://www.limra.com/en/research/research-abstracts-public/2018/2018-insurance-barometer/.

9. Trisha Rozas and Neal Matthews, "Data and the Cloud: Two Key Drivers of the Insurance Industry's Future," Cloud Technology Partners, July 26, 2019, https://www.cloudtp.com/doppler/data-and-the-cloud-two-key-drivers-of-the-insurance-industrys-future/.

10. Conor Donegan, "State of the Connected Consumer Report Outlines Changing Standards for Customer Engagement, June 12, 2019, https://www.salesforce.com/company/news-press/stories/2019/06/061219-g/.

11. Katie Dwyer, "5 Ways Technology Is Reshaping the Future of Insurance," Risk & Insurance, April 19, 2019, https://riskandinsurance.com/5-ways-technology-is-reshaping-insurance/.

12. "What Should Insurers Do Today to Prepare for Tomorrow? US and America's Insurance Outlook 2019," Ernst & Young LLP, 2018, https://www.ey.com/Publication/vwLUAssets/EY-us-and-americas-insurance-outlook-2019/$FILE/EY-us-and-americas-insurance-outlook-2019.pdf.

13. Peer Insight Ventures, "2020 Insurance Trends: Good Vibrations for Agile Insurers," IoT for all, December 19, 2019. https://www.iotforall.com/internet-of-things-and-insurance-industry/.

14. "Financial Services and Insurance," Infosys: Insights, https://www.infosys.com/services/cloud/insights/cloud-financial-services-insurance-industry.html

15. "Live Enterprise: Sustainability Report 2018–2019," Infosys, https://www.infosys.com/sustainability/Documents/infosys-sustainability-report-2018-19.pdf.

16. Peter Vahle, "Kohl's Increases Foot Traffic by Accepting Amazon Returns," eMarketer, May 10, 2019, https://www.emarketer.com/content/kohl-s-increases-foot-traffic-by-accepting-amazon-returns-9/.

17. "Amazon Partnership Delivers for Kohl's," Earnest Research, April 3, 2019, https://medium.com/earnest-research/amazon-partnership-delivers-for-kohls-4d59207ee9a1.

18. Hayley Peterson, "Kohl's CEO Said Amazon Returns Boosted Traffic—And Shows the Jump Could Be as High as 24%," *Business Insider*, https://www.businessinsider.com/amazon-returns-help-boost-kohls-stores-shopper-traffic-2019-8.

19. "JD Power: P&C Insurance Industry Insight Brief," *Insurance Journal*, April 26, 2019, https://www.insurancejournal.com/research/research/j-d-power-pc-insurance-industry-insight-brief/.

20. "Insurers Come Up Short for Independent Agents Despite Critical Role Agents Play in Driving Business, J.D. Power Finds," J.D. Power press release, January 31, 2019, https://www.jdpower.com/business/press-releases/2019-us-independent-insurance-agent-satisfaction-study.

21. Lisa Shidler, "Guess Who's Moving into the RIA neighborhood? State Farm Asks Thousands of Insurance Brokers to Get Financial Planning Credentials, Sources Say," RIABiz, October 25, 2018, https://riabiz.com/a/2018/10/25/guess-whos-moving-into-the-ria-neighborhood-state-farm-asks-thousands-of-insurance-brokers-to-get-financial-planning-credentials-sources-sa.

22. "There's No Need to Fly Solo on Your Finances," State Farm, https://www.statefarm.com/finances.

23. "AXA's $15.3B Deal to Buy XL Group Leads to S&P CreditWatch Negative Status," Carrier Management, March 7, 2018, https://www.carriermanagement.com/news/2018/03/07/176386.htm.

24. John Hewitt Jones, "AXA XL to Cut 7.5% of Workforce," *The Insurance Insider*, February 12, 2019, https://www.insuranceinsider.com/articles/124651/axa-xl-to-cut-75-of-workforce.

25. "Direct and Independent Agent Sales Channels Become Ground Zero in Auto Insurers' Battle to Win New Customers, J.D. Power Finds," J.D. Power press release, April 25, 2019, https://www.jdpower.com/business/press-releases/2019-us-insurance-shopping-study.

26. "Financial advice made simple," https://www.apple.com/business/success-stories/

27. See www.goodfetch.com.

28. James Melton, "Millennials Now Do 60% of Their Shopping Online," Digital Commerce 360, March 26, 2019, https://www.digitalcommerce360.com/2019/03/26/millennials-online-shopping/.

29. Ibid.; "2018 Insurance Barometer."

30. "Millennial Business Owners More Likely to Work with Agents," *Insurance News*, December 11, 2018, https://insurancenewsnet.com/oarticle/millennial-business-owners-more-likely-to-work-with-agents#.XXbCKyV7l-0.

31. Marshall Hargrave, "Insurtech," Investopedia, August 20, 2019, https://www.investopedia.com/terms/i/insurtech.asp.

32. "Digital Ecosystems for Insurers: Opportunities through the Internet of Things," McKinsey & Company, February 2019, https://www.mckinsey.com/industries/financial-services/our-insights/digital-ecosystems-for-insurers-opportunities-through-the-internet-of-things.

33. "2019 Insurance Industry Outlook, "Deloitte, https://www2.deloitte.com/us/en/pages/financial-services/articles/insurance-industry-outlook.html.

34. Chip and Dan Heath, "The Power of Moments: Why Certain Experiences Have Extraordinary Impact," *Fast Company*, October 3, 2017, https://www.fastcompany.com/40472116/the-power-of-moments-why-certain-experiences-have-extraordinary-impact.

35. Conor Donegan, "State of the Connected Consumer Report Outlines Changing Standards for Customer Engagement," Salesforce, June 12, 2019, https://www.salesforce.com/company/news-press/stories/2019/06/061219-g/.

36. Shep Hyken, "Customer Experience Is the New Brand, *Forbes*, July 15, 2018, https://www.forbes.com/sites/shephyken/2018/07/15/customer-experience-is-the-new-brand/#48002e917f52.

37. "Experience Is Everything: Here's How to Get It Right," PwC, 2018, https://www.pwc.com/us/en/advisory-services/publications/consumer-intelligence-series/pwc-consumer-intelligence-series-customer-experience.pdf.

38. To get a copy of my book, *Discussion Partner*, go to Amazon.com or my website, wwwkorsgaden.com.

39. "NAIC Releases 2018 Market Share Data," NAIC, https://naic.org/Releases/2019_docs/naic_releases_2018_market_share_data.htm.

40. Steven MacDonald, "Why Customer Complaints Are Good for Your Business," Super Office, October 7, 2019, https://www.superoffice.com/blog/customer-complaints-good-for-business/.

41. "Types of Selling," Lumen, Boundless Marketing, https://courses.lumenlearning.com/boundless-marketing/chapter/types-of-selling/.

42. *Discussion Partner*, pp. 29–30.

43. Ibid.

44. Nikki Gilliland, "17 Stats That Show Why CX Is So Important," Econsultancy, December 12, 2019, https://econsultancy.com/17-stats-that-show-why-cx-is-so-important/.

45. "The Ongoing Evolution of Organic: Why It's Popular and Where It's Heading," Cathy Siegner, FoodDive, March 19, 2018, https://www.fooddive.com/news/the-ongoing-evolution-of-organic-why-its-popular-and-where-its-heading/519268/

46.. "Buying Insurance Leads," Insurance Leads Guide, https://insurance-leadsguide.com/buying-insurance-leads/.

47. Aja Frost, "75 Key Sales Statistics That'll Help You Sell Smarter in 2019," Hubspot, June 3, 2019, https://blog.hubspot.com/sales/sales-statistics.

48. Tyson Quick, "What Is Personalized Marketing & How Can You Excel at It?" Instapage, June 14, 2019, https://instapage.com/blog/personalized-marketing.

49. "Making Learning a Part of Everyday Work," Josh Bersin and Marc Zao-Sanders, *Harvard Business Review*, February 19, 2019, https://hbr.org/2019/02/making-learning-a-part-of-everyday-work

50. "Stop Exceeding Customer Expectations: To Create Immediately Loyalty Do This Instead," Mareo McCracken, *Inc.*, January 9, 2018, https://www.inc.com/mareo-mccracken/stop-exceeding-customer-expectations-to-create-immediate-loyalty-do-this-instead.html

51. Patrick Lee and Mac Donald, "The Future's So Bright, I Gotta Wear Shades," Warner Chappell Music, Inc., The Bicycle Music Company.

52. "Omnichannel Marketing," MediaBeacon, https://www.mediabeacon.com/en/landingpages/omnichannel-marketing-what-is-it?utm_source=google&utm_campaign=na-dam&utm_medium=cpc&utm_term=utm_term&utm_content=what-is-omnichannel&utm_source=-Google&utm_medium=&utm_campaign=&utm_term=what%20is%20omnichannel&matchtype=p&device=c&gclid=EAIaIQobCh-MIgqin2ZrH5AIVjcBkCh09zASuEAAYASAAEgIGk_D_BwE.

53. Branwell Moffat, "Ominichannel vs. Multichannel: What's the Difference and Who Is Doing It?" *The Future of Customer Engagement and Commerce*, September 13, 2017, https://www.the-future-of-commerce.com/2017/09/13/omnichannel-vs-multichannel/.

54. Barbara Friedberg, "Simplify Your Investing Life with Fewer Accounts," *US News & World Report*, May 16, 2018, https://money.usnews.com/investing/investing-101/articles/2018-05-16/5-reasons-to-consolidate-your-investing-accounts.

ACKNOWLEDGMENTS

I would like to thank my family, friends, and colleagues who have helped guide and shape my thinking over many years. They have supported me in the past, they continue to encourage me today, and their belief in my future is a great treasure.

I would also like to thank my editors, writing collaborators, and business associates who have helped me bring my concepts to life in this book.

Most of all, I'm grateful to God for all the blessings and opportunities He gives me. "With God all things are possible" (Matthew 19:26).

ABOUT THE AUTHOR

TROY KORSGADEN
PRESIDENT AND CONSULTANT,
KORSGADEN INTERNATIONAL
VISALIA, CALIFORNIA
TROY@KORSGADEN.COM
KORSGADEN.COM

Troy Korsgaden is the principal of Korsgaden International, which specializes in global marketing, distribution, agency building, and technology strategies for many of the world's largest insurance carriers and financial services companies. He is a highly sought-after insurance and financial services consultant, speaker, and the author of seven books.

Troy is passionate about helping the insurance industry and its representatives wake up to the radical transformation taking place in the industry. He creates the necessary tools and road maps for building success in the rapidly changing insurance and financial services landscape.

A widely respected expert in personal distribution and other methods, Troy trains corporate insurance and financial services leaders on customer service, change management, and transformational work, among many other critical issues impacting insurance carriers and financial services companies.

He helps those in the industry learn how to communicate more effectively with their teams and consumers so that consumers develop a higher appreciation for the value of insurance products and their insurance advisor relationships. Korsgaden

International provides turnkey approaches using leading technologies and management tools that create fluency and seamlessness in product delivery and customer service.

Hundreds of thousands of insurance and financial services executives, agents, brokers, and staff members have been inspired and empowered by Troy's seminars and guidance for more than 30 years.

Troy consults most major companies in the insurance and financial services industry in some capacity, working with large carriers, both in property & casualty and in financial services. He also serves as a subject-matter expert in the area of technology and how it applies in the backroom for carriers as well as their distribution.

He is considered an expert in distribution strategy, in both personal distribution and other methods. He also provides consulting to business owners and corporate leaders on topics including customer service, change management, and transformational work. He advises leaders at all levels of organizations on global marketing strategies.

In terms of personal production, over his career, Troy has won every production and quality service award offered by the carrier he represents and was the top-ranked agent in the nation twice. He has been a member of a top-producing group for that carrier for 21 consecutive years, an elite honor accomplished by less than ½ of 1 percent of all 15,000+ representatives within the United States.

Since his humble beginnings in establishing the Korsgaden/ Jansma Farmers Insurance Agency in 1983, Troy has been exceptionally driven and committed to help clients determine the best options for their insurance coverage.

ABOUT KORSGADEN INSURANCE CARRIER CONSULTING

Troy Korsgaden has a proven track record for advising insurance carrier executives and distribution leaders on growing sales and increasing retention.

As an insurance industry expert, Troy is a highly-sought-after consultant for both large and small insurance carriers. Profitability hinges on good systems, and Troy helps carrier executives and distribution leaders set up systems that work for IT, marketing, distribution, recruiting, and training.

Troy specializes in creating continuity programs and implementing the right protocols for sales, follow-up, and relationship building at the agency level to significantly increase productivity. The goal is to keep your agents working at maximum efficiency your and agency producing outstanding results.

By continually improving your internal processes, you stay ahead of the competition. Troy excels in developing recruiting and training systems that bring in the right people, building marketing and distribution systems for companies of all sizes, executing sales strategies that support rapid and sustained growth, and employing measurement tools that gauge the effectiveness of both programs and people.

Troy will assist you in finding your place in the market and ensuring that your agents and staff are well-prepared to take advantage of it. He works alongside carrier organizations to develop a comprehensive productivity strategy to help you create strong agencies that provide maximum return on investment.

His consulting approach focuses not just on strategy, but also on practical steps to reach your goals. Troy seeks to understand your objectives and what makes you different. Then he will work directly with your corporate teams to improve operations and distribution strategy. He is dedicated to creating long-term relationships with the carriers he serves.

RESOURCES

In *Discussion Partner,* Troy Korsgaden introduces the concept of professional alliances and explains how they benefit each person involved. This radical transformation is already taking place in the insurance industry. Follow his advice and earn the right to be trusted by existing clients and new prospects. Eventually, all of us will become multiline reps, selling a wide range of products and services. To compete in the market, we have to excel in providing unrivaled service. Nothing else will do.

His book, *Inflection Point,* assumes the importance of Discussion Partners and shows how to apply these principles in our rapidly changing industry.

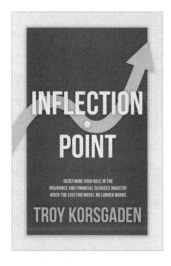

An inflection point occurs at a critical moment when the situation calls for new thinking and a different strategy. In this book, Troy Korsgaden makes the convincing case that this moment has arrived for the insurance industry. Previous assumptions about the way we do business are no longer accurate. Delay will be devastating. If we don't see the need to change—and change now—many of us will lose customers . . . and perhaps lose our businesses.

Enjoying a balanced life—one infused with peace, meaningful relationships, and a compelling purpose—seems like a pipedream to many of us. If we're dedicated to achieving our full potential in our careers, our home life and health often suffer. But we're often afraid that devoting too much time to our families, mental health, and physical fitness will cause us to fall behind at work. We live in this tension every day. In this book, Troy Korsgaden is honest about his struggles to achieve this kind of balance. He has found the keys to success and sanity and shares his insights on his lifelong process to apply these principles.